Cross Over to HTML5 Game Development

Use Your Programming Experience to Create Mobile Games

Zarrar Chishti

Apress®

Cross Over to HTML5 Game Development: Use Your Programming Experience to Create Mobile Games

Zarrar Chishti
Glasgow, United Kingdom

ISBN-13 (pbk): 978-1-4842-3290-3   ISBN-13 (electronic): 978-1-4842-3291-0
https://doi.org/10.1007/978-1-4842-3291-0

Library of Congress Control Number: 2017961309

Cover image designed by Freepik

Managing Director: Welmoed Spahr
Editorial Director: Todd Green
Acquisitions Editor: Aaron Black
Development Editor: James Markham
Technical Reviewer: Massimo Nardone
Coordinating Editor: Jessica Vakili
Copy Editor: Kim Burton-Weisman
Compositor: SPi Global
Indexer: SPi Global
Artist: SPi Global

Distributed to the book trade worldwide by Springer Science+Business Media New York, 233 Spring Street, 6th Floor, New York, NY 10013. Phone 1-800-SPRINGER, fax (201) 348-4505, e-mail orders-ny@springer-sbm.com, or visit www.springeronline.com. Apress Media, LLC is a California LLC and the sole member (owner) is Springer Science + Business Media Finance Inc (SSBM Finance Inc). SSBM Finance Inc is a **Delaware** corporation.

For information on translations, please e-mail rights@apress.com, or visit http://www.apress.com/rights-permissions.

Apress titles may be purchased in bulk for academic, corporate, or promotional use. eBook versions and licenses are also available for most titles. For more information, reference our Print and eBook Bulk Sales web page at http://www.apress.com/bulk-sales.

Any source code or other supplementary material referenced by the author in this book is available to readers on GitHub via the book's product page, located at www.apress.com/978-1-4842-3290-3. For more detailed information, please visit http://www.apress.com/source-code.

Printed on acid-free paper

Table of Contents

About the Author

Zarrar Chishti is a software and games development consultant with over 500 games developed for companies around the world. He is sought after to advise on the development of viral games for major marketing campaigns. His consultancy and development firm include prestigious companies such as Turner Media, British Airways and Channel 4 among the many clients that keep coming back when a new product or service is being launched.

After graduating from Glasgow University in 1996 with a prestigious joint honors degree in Software Engineering, Zarrar contracted as a software developer in both London and L.A. for 5 years. In 2001 he opened his own software firm in Glasgow and within 2 years was employing 10 staff. This was to grow to 30 in 2005 when he began to offer games development to his clients.

One of the most notable game projects Zarrar has produced includes an interactive comic for the popular Ben 10 TV series. The project was a notable success that took his firm 10 months to deliver. It was rolled out in over 25 countries in localized language editions. Other projects include building a series of games for the ever popular Big Brother TV franchise and an employee training game for Legal and General.

About the Author

About the Technical Reviewer

Massimo Nardone has more than 22 years of experiences in security, web/mobile development, and cloud and IT architecture. His true IT passions are security and Android.

He has programmed and taught how to program with Android, Perl, PHP, Java, VB, Python, C/C++ and MySQL for more than 20 years.

He holds a master's degree in computing science from the University of Salerno, Italy.

He has worked as a project manager, software engineer, research engineer, chief security architect, information security manager, PCI/SCADA auditor and senior lead IT security/cloud/SCADA architect for many years.

His technical skills include security, Android, cloud, Java, MySQL, Drupal, Cobol, Perl, web and mobile development, MongoDB, D3, Joomla, Couchbase, C/C++, WebGL, Python, Pro Rails, Django CMS, Jekyll, Scratch, and more.

He currently works as chief information security office (CISO) for Cargotec Oyj.

He worked as visiting lecturer and supervisor for exercises at the Networking Laboratory of the Helsinki University of Technology (Aalto University). He holds four international patents (PKI, SIP, SAML, and Proxy areas).

Massimo has reviewed more than 40 IT books for various publishing companies. He is the coauthor of *Pro Android Games* (Apress, 2015).

Acknowledgments

To Pops - you were an amazing dad who has left a massive hole in our lives.

To my closest friend, who has been (and continues to be) there for me at the times when it matters the most: my brother Ibrar. Thank you to my parents, who gave me the most amazing education and start to life. My one constant and partner in crime, my wife Sadia. My son, whom I am so proud of (incidentally, he was my initial editor for the book) and my "janno-jaan" daughters: Sara, Aisha, and Rushda. I would be in a tremendous amount of trouble if I did not also acknowledge Bella, our Bengal cat.

I would like to say a heartfelt thank you to my agent, Carole. You agreed to represent me, despite my thick Scottish accent! Your guidance and patience at the start will always be remembered and appreciated. Also, thank you to the awesome and gorgeous team at Apress: Aaron and Jessica. I had a great time working with you both and you made this "noob" feel like part of the team.

I want to thank two people who have inspired me to write books. My Latin teacher Mr. Temperely and my favorite author of all time, David Blixt. I would also like send my love and appreciation to all my staff, both past and present: Alasdair, George, Paul (the Great), Les, and Claire. Also, my thanks to those clients that gave me my initial start despite having little or no experience.

Finally, I would like to thank the nurses and doctors at Monklands Haematology department who looked after my wife, Sadia. I will always remember your commitment, passion, and support that you gave to her. Thank you for sending her home to us.

Preface

Welcome to the wonderful world of HTML5 game development. Are you looking for a new challenge or looking to expand your current skill set? Then get ready to start your journey. This book has been written with a simple goal in mind: to provide the means for anyone to develop their first HTML5 game.

This is a great time to break into the most lucrative game development platform in the world. The global demand for the HTML5 game development platform has expanded so quickly that it is currently crying out for seasoned developers from more traditional environments to cross over. Never before has there been such a widely accepted platform by literally every manufacturer and operating system. This, in turn, has convinced marketing departments to move away from traditional platforms, such as dedicated mobile apps, for the more widely accepted HTML5 format.

In short, there has never been a better time for a seasoned IT programmer to cross over and capitalize in this lucrative market with their much sought-after talents and experience.

I have spent the last five years training developers from a wide range of programming disciplines to cross-train in HTML5 game development. Whatever your vocation, whether it be an application databases systems developer or a professional web developer, with this book you will learn to evolve your current coding skills to enable you to become eligible for the biggest gaming platform in the world.

From the first chapter, you immediately see encouraging results as you power through a challenging and fun project that has been uniquely designed and developed for this book.

Why This Book

This book was written with a simple goal in mind: to help seasoned programmers from other disciplines to cross over to HTML5 game development.

No apps need to be purchased. No special hardware or software is required. As long as you have a simple computer with Internet access, you can start today.

How quickly you build this game is entirely up to you. For each major step we come across, you can decide to either study the technical aspects or skip ahead to the next step. Either way, by the end of this book, you will have a playable game to show off to friends and family.

This book is perfect for anyone that just wants to roll up their sleeves and start developing a game for themselves. I believe that by the end of this book, you will be in a far better position to make a decision on whether you want to invest your time and money in becoming a qualified games developer.

What You Will Need

Any computer will do.

- You do **not** need a super-fast computer

- You do **not** need an expensive IDE installed

- You do **not** need the latest graphics card

You can build this game using the computer/laptop that you already have—as long as it switches on and you can run the already installed Notepad program (if you are using Windows) or TextEdit (if you are on an Apple Mac).

What about your phone or tablet? Technically, it is possible; however, it is not ideal because the operating environment is not suited to coding (i.e., typing). If you do wish to use these devices, then you may wish to invest in a Bluetooth keyboard and an external memory card.

How to Use This Book

During this project, I have spent a great deal of my time minimizing the amount of code that you need to write. However, I had to balance this with making code that was still readable, which means that in occasional instances of this book, you will find some lengthy portions of code to write. I do apologize for this; however, keep in mind that you will be able to reuse the code in your next project.

The following icons appear in the book.

In this section, you will see the actual code that will need to be written. It is important to ensure that you copy the code exactly as it is written.

On most occasions, you will only need to write the lines that are written in bold. Also, the lines of code that existed before but have just been modified are in red.

Further Information

In this section, you will see interesting facts and explanations of the code that has just been written. If you wish to build on your coding knowledge as you proceed, then you will find a great source of information here. However, feel free to ignore this section if you just want to get on with building your game.

Not Working?

Did something go wrong? Did the code you just wrote not work? Not to worry. You will find common (and some not so common) mistakes here with solutions on how to fix them.

CHAPTER 1

Introduction

*"If you have a garden and a library,
you have everything you need."*

Marcus Tullius Cicero
(106 BC – 43 BC)

```
var replaceWord1 = str.replace("garden", "computer");
var replaceWord2 = str.replace("a library", "time");
```

I have been developing software since 1996 and I have developed games for small and large companies for over a decade now. Like any form of development in the real world, you need to know why you are building the game before you think of coding strategies and build processes. In the gaming world, this comes in the form of the game's story. This includes the background, reasons to play, and the goals of the game.

Introducing Our Game: Space Zombies

So here is our story, which we will develop into a game.

 Hi. My name is Ace Star. The year is 2107. For the last three months, I have been stationed as a security guard on the only moon of planet ZC636, which is in the Andromeda Galaxy. In addition to me and a group of dignitaries from Earth, there is a group of about 500 top scientists stationed here to work on secret experiments.

1

© Zarrar Chishti 2017
Z. Chishti, *Cross Over to HTML5 Game Development*,
https://doi.org/10.1007/978-1-4842-3291-0_1

I need your help.

Last night, there was an explosion in one of the labs. A gas was released that turned all the scientists in the lab into zombies.

I have positioned myself outside the only doors of the colony's main building. The other survivors are safely inside. I am the last line of defense before help arrives from Earth.

I discovered that our weapons are useless against the zombies. While running out of the labs, however, I found a new, experimental weapon.

It seems to do the trick.

I can hear them coming. Are you ready?

Let's have a look at a few of the graphics that we will use for the development.

	This is the background image for our game. It will fill the screen by stretching out both horizontally and vertically. Our zombies will spawn from where the ground meets the sky. Once spawned, they will come toward us, growing bigger.
	Say hello to Professor Z, our average zombie. In terms of speed, he is not very fast and he does not suddenly sprint to the front. He simply heads toward you at his own leisurely speed! In terms of our weapon shots, he will not be too hard or too easy to "neutralize." It takes two zaps to get him.
	Say *ciao* to Belladonna, our fastest zombie. Keep an eye on her because she will appear one minute and then suddenly sprint to the front. She will not be too hard to neutralize, however. One zap will get her.

	Finally, this is Brad, our heavyweight zombie. Unfortunately, due to all of those hours lifting weights, he is slower than the average zombie. He takes his time to gain speed once he spawns. He will be harder to neutralize, however. It takes three zaps to get him.
	This is the experimental weapon that our hero found in one of the labs. When fired, it zaps out a special liquid, which when successfully administered, encases the zombie in an air bubble. It will need to be reloaded often.
	This is our Reload button. From a game-design point of view, it adds another dimension to the gameplay.
	This is our game's logo. We will not see it until the last chapter of the book, when we embed our game.
	This is the box that we will embed into our game. Initially, you see the game span the entire screen. Near the end, however, we look at embedding the code into this box.
	This is the background image that we use in the final chapter. The background is the main image used when we build a dedicated web page to embed our game into.

The following is a screenshot of the finished game.

Setting up Your Work Environment

This section discusses how to set up your work environment.

Part 1: Setting up Our Folders

You need to create a work folder where all of your work files can be stored. This makes it easier to distinguish your work files from all the others on your computer. So first, create a root (or master) folder called My_Work_ Files in the C drive.

Once you have your root folder, the next step is to create the subfolders that you will need for the game. Create four folders inside My_Work_Files. Name the folders as follows:

- CSS

- Images

- Raw Images

- js

Your folder should look like the following screenshot.

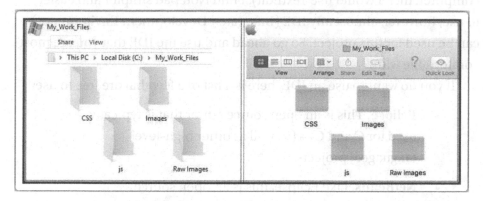

The CSS folder will hold special code files that help structure the design of the game. All the files in this folder will end in .css.

The js folder will hold all of our JavaScript files, which will form the engine for our game. They will contain commands and instructions that will control what happens in our game. All the files in this folder will end in .js.

The Images folder, as the name suggests, will contain all the image or media files that we will need for the game.

The Raw Images folder will not technically be used for raw images. In our case, we will use this folder as special temporary housing for all of our media. We will move them into the Images folder when we need them.

Part 2: Setting up Our Files

For the purposes of this book, I will use Notepad (if you are using an Apple computer, then I would use TextEdit). I find Notepad simpler and easier to use; however, almost any IDE (Integrated Development Environment) can be used for this project. So go ahead and use the IDE that you are most comfortable with.

If you do want to use an IDE, here is a list of a few that are free to use:

- **Eclipse**. This is an open source editor that is typically used for C and C++ (as well as other high-level languages) projects.

- **NetBeans**. Like Eclipse, this is an open source editor; however, it comes bundled with a plethora of development frameworks.

- **Aptana**. A very popular IDE among web developers, it can be plugged into Eclipse. Typically used for HTML projects.

- **CodeRun**. This is a slightly unusual choice in that it runs on a browser (i.e., it is a web-based IDE). Personally, I find it excellent for last-minute fixes when at a remote location.

- **Visual Studio Community**. This is free for individual programmers and comes packed with all the amazing features that you will find in Visual Studio Professional series.

Although using an IDE has its benefits, I think that it is worth keeping in mind this excellent quote about using IDEs for multiple languages:

"Although many IDEs can handle more than one language, few do it well. Plus, it's likely overkill if you are just getting started."

Now that the folders are set up, let's create the files that you will use to develop the game.

First, you need to create a `default.html` file. If you are using an IDE, click File ➤ Create New and select HTML. If you are using Notepad, open a new file and save it as `default.html`.

Your folder should now look like this:

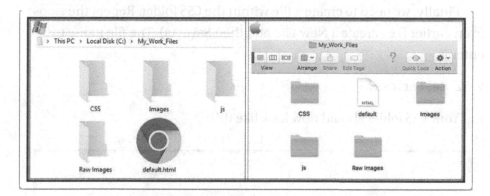

Now, we need to create files within some of the folders we created. Double-click the `js` folder. Repeat the preceding steps (i.e., create a New File and then Save As). The following are the file names to enter:

- > `SZ_main.js`
- > `SZ_movement.js`
- > `SZ_setupContent.js`
- > `SZ_SS.js`
- > `SZ_touch.js`
- > `SZ_zombie_movement.js`

Your js folder should now look like this:

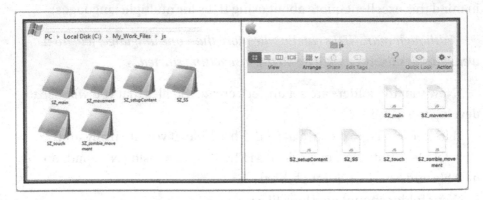

Finally, we need to create a file within the CSS folder. Repeat the steps from earlier (i.e., create a New File and then Save As). The file name to enter is

> SZ_master.css.

Your CSS folder should now look like this:

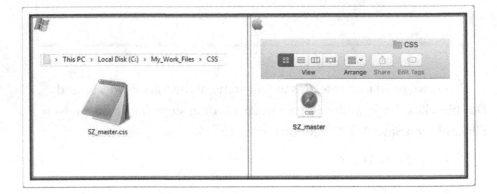

Further Information

We need our files to work across the worldwide network successfully, so we should try to keep to the standardized naming conventions.

It is best to avoid character spaces in file names. Technically, this is acceptable in local environments (Apple and Windows OS), however, character spaces are not recognized by other systems. Ideally, use an underscore or a hyphen character to separate words within file names.

Do not use any special characters, such as !, ?, %, #, or /. It is best to limit file names to underscores, numbers, and letters.

For this project, you will notice that I try to consistently start all of my file names with SZ_. This is because they are the initials for the name of the game—**S**pace **Z**ombies. It is important to be consistent and descriptive in naming and organizing files so that it is obvious where to find specific data and what the files contain.

By naming your files in a meaningful manner, you increase your chances of finding those files in the future and knowing what information they contain. When you come to develop new games, you will easily be able to locate Space Zombie files by searching for all files starting with SZ_.

Finally, it is good practice to keep file names as short as possible. Apart from adding to the size of the file, it also makes them easier to remember six months down the line.

Hosting and Media Files

As long as the files remain on your hard drive (the files and folders created earlier), you will be able to test the game comfortably on your computer. This is certainly okay for budding developers starting out.

Nonetheless, at some point when you have developed several games, you may wish to showcase them for all to see and play.

To do this, you need to upload your files to a server computer. A server is essentially a computer that is connected to the Internet.

Part 1: Your Computer vs. Hosting Servers

You need to open an account with a server computer. If you do a Google search for "server hosting free trial," you have several options available. If you are still unsure, please do not hesitate to message me on Twitter @zarrarchishti.

The following is a short list of available hosting options.

Dedicated Server

This is the most expensive option. Essentially, you own the computer that is connected to the Internet. This is only an option if you are either a huge company or a reseller.

10

Shared Server

This is generally the most economical option for hosting. It is very much
for people like you, who are renting a piece of the server. The main
advantage is the ridiculously low cost, of course. However, as your game
development expertise increases, you may find this option to be limiting
and unfit for your specific needs.

Cloud Hosting

Whereas the prior two options rely on one physical computer, cloud
hosting allows an unlimited number of computers to act as one system.

Part 2: Download the Media for Your Project

The media files (image and sound files) used in the project are available
for you to download.

Open your Internet browser and go to the following URL:

`http://zarrarchishtiauthor.com/downloads/`

Click the Download button. This will initiate a download. The browser
will let you know when it has completed. Navigate to your download folder
and locate the downloaded file.

It should be a file called `raw_media_1.rar`. Now you need to extract the
files from this zipped file in a new folder called `Raw Media`. Double-click
this folder and you will see the following four folders:

- > `Images`
- > `JS`
- > `sounds`
- > `html_web`

First, copy all four folders to your Raw Images folder, which is in the My_Work_Files folder.

At this stage, we are only interested in the files inside the JS folder. As we progress through the game, we will go back to the other folders and copy the files as needed. Double-click the JS folder (in the Raw Images folder). Using the same technique as before to copy files, go ahead and copy all the files, and then paste them into your own js folder (in the My_Work_Files folder).

Your js folder (in the My_Work_Files folder) should now look like this:

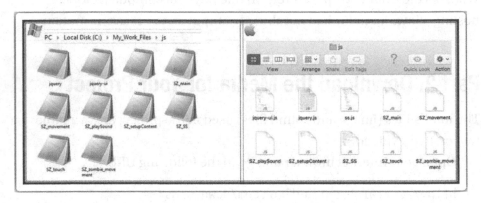

That's it for now! We have successfully set up our game development environment. We are now ready to start coding our game!

Further Information

The files we copied over from the JS folder are special JavaScript programs that we can use for our game. Imagine a library of code maintained by companies like Google that contain functions that make our lives easier.

The files—for instance, jQuery—are fast, small, and feature-rich JavaScript libraries. Together they make things like HTML document traversal and manipulation, event handling, animation, and AJAX much simpler with an easy-to-use API that works across a multitude of browsers.

When using a library such as this, we do not need to ever worry about how they work. All we need to know is what they do so that we can decide whether we want to use them in our games.

Another advantage of using libraries such as jQuery is that it runs exactly the same in all major browsers, including Internet Explorer 6! So no need to worry about cross-browser issues.

Usually, we link to these files directly from the source servers. The advantage of doing it this way is that we always get the latest copy of the code when running our game. However, since we want to be able to play the game offline, let's choose to download them into our local folders.

1) In  Windows, did the option to Extract Here appear? If not, you need to download WinRAR from the following:

   `http://www.win-rar.com/download.html`

2) Are you using a laptop? To right-click, you need to first click `ctrl`   and then click the mousepad.

3) When downloading the media files, did you receive a message from your browser warning you that the download is not commonly used and may be dangerous? If yes, this is because I chose to WINRAR rather than to WINZIP the file. The files are not dangerous. You may click Keep; however, feel free to run a virus check on the folder before opening.

CHAPTER 2

In the Beginning, There Was HTML

"Nine people can't make a baby in a month."

Fred Brooks

HTML is a mark-up language that is used to develop web sites. So why do we need this for our game? It is best to imagine HTML as the skeleton or bone structure of our game.

As a side note, once you have completed this chapter, you will have not only started your journey into game development, but also web development!

Hello World

During my 20 years of programming, I have learned many programming languages. The first project that I always work on is learning how to output the words "Hello World." to the screen. I bet that you follow this tradition too, so let's develop a "Hello World" page in HTML.

Open the `default.html` file in Notepad or TextEdit in the `My_Work_Files` folder using the same program or IDE that you used in the "Part 2: Setting up Our Files" section in Chapter 1.

15

© Zarrar Chishti 2017
Z. Chishti, *Cross Over to HTML5 Game Development*,
https://doi.org/10.1007/978-1-4842-3291-0_2

When the file opens, it should be completely blank. Type the following lines:

```
<html>
 <head>
 </head>
 <body>
  <div id="SZ_maincontent">
  Hello World.
  </div>
 </body>
</html>
```

Navigate to the menu, click File and then click on Save. You can now close this file. Navigate back to the menu, click File, and then click Exit/Close.

Are you ready to test your very first program?

Go back to the My_Work_Files folder and double-click the default.html file. This should open in your default Internet browser; for example, Microsoft Edge, Google Chrome, or Safari.

The page that opens up on the browser should be a completely blank page with the words "Hello World." displayed in the top-left corner. Excellent. Our program works and we have written our first piece of code!

Obviously, this is nowhere near a game yet. All the same, persevere with the work between now and that point. Rest assured, by the end of this book, we will have developed the entire game. It will most certainly be worth it. And you will be learning a lot of different techniques to get you started on your journey to developing a suite of games!

HTML stands for Hypertext Markup Language. *Hypertext* is the method by which you navigate around the Internet. *Hyper* just means it is not linear, or you can go to any place on the Web by clicking links. *Markup* is what HTML tags do to the text inside them. They mark it as a certain type of text (bolded text, for example).

Here are the descriptions of each of the tags that you just coded:

- `<html> </html>` This is required at the start and at the end of every new web page. Everything inside these two tags constitutes the contents of your page.

- `<head> </head>` The contents of the head tag include the title for the page, scripts, styles, and meta information.

- `<body> </body>` All the visual contents of our web page, such as text, hyperlinks, and images, are contained within this tag.

- `<div> </div>` This defines a particular section of our page. It is best to think of the div tags as containers. It is not unusual to have div tags within bigger div tags.

You will notice that the closing tags are basically the same as the opening tags, with a forward slash preceding it; for example, `</div>` signals that you are closing that particular tag.

Please remember that every tag must be closed.

Background Image

The game's background image does not change, move, or interact with the gameplay. It provides a backdrop for all the various elements that will be controlled by the actual game.

First, go to the `images` folder in the `Raw  Images` folder of the `My_Work_Files` folder. Locate the file called `SZ_background_image.jpg`. You need to copy this file over to your `Images` folder, which should then look like this:

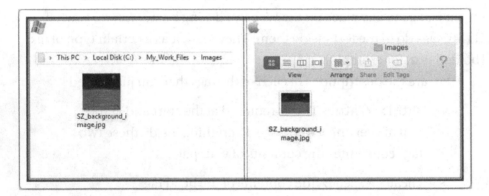

Let's reopen the `default.html` file. Remove the "Hello World" line by selecting the line and clicking Delete/Backspace. Now type the following new line (all the new text is in bold):

```
<html>
 <head>
 </head>
 <body>
  <div id="SZ_maincontent">
   <img id="SZo_0" src="images/SZ_background_image.jpg" />
  </div>
 </body>
</html>
```

Save the file and then close it. Go back to the My_Work_Files folder and double-click the default.html file.

By using the <img> tag, we have defined a background image for our page. It is important to note that the image is not technically inserted into our HTML page; rather, the background image has been linked to our HTML page. The <img> tag has created a holding space for the background image.

The "Hello World" text should have disappeared, and the background image is now in its place. It does not look like it's covering the screen. Do not worry about that. We will align and resize our images in the next chapter.

Further Information

In this section, you came across the <img> tag, which is used when you want to place an image in your web page.

Inside the <img> tag, you will notice

id="SZ0_0"

As it suggests, this is the ID for the image tag. This ID is used when we start coding in JavaScript in Chapter 4.

Also, you will have noticed the src tag:

src="images/SZ_background_image.jpg"

src, which stands for "source," allows you to specify the location of the image. Earlier in this section, we placed SZ_background_image.jpg in the images folder. So as you can see, the src is the exact location and the name of the image file.

Now, let's think back to the previous section, when I said that you always need to include closing tags. I ended the section by stating that all tags must be closed. However, the code that we just wrote did not include `</img>`. So, did I forget?

What I did there was close our tag within the opening tag. Note that at the end of our `img` tag, there is a forward slash before the `>`. This is another way to close tags if you do not need add elements outwith what is written in the opening tag itself.

Let's analyze our line of code:

```
<img id="SZ0_0" src="images/SZ_background_image.jpg" />
```

We have managed to put all the information concerning our image inside the opening tag. There was no additional information required; therefore, we can close our tag by writing `/>`.

In case you are wondering, the following is just as valid:

```
<img id="SZ0_0" src="images/SZ_background_image.jpg" ></img>
```

Adding the Rest of the Images

The following images also need to be added to our HTML page:

- `SZ_gun.png`

- `SZ_reload.png`

- `SZ_score.png`

There will be many more images by the time we finish the game; however, this is all that we need at this stage.

As before, go into the images folder in the Raw Images folder of the My_Work_Files folder. Locate the three new .png files and copy them over to your Images folder, which should then look like this:

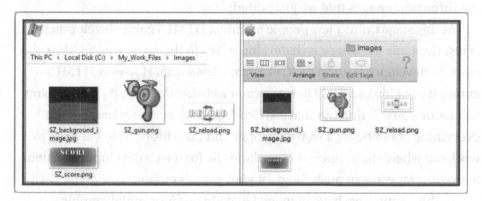

Now, reopen the default.html file and type the following new lines (all the new text is in bold):

```
<html>
 <head>
 </head>
 <body>
  <div id="SZ_maincontent">
   <img id="SZO_0" src="images/SZ_background_image.jpg" />
   <img id="SZO_1" src="images/SZ_gun.png" />
   <img id="SZO_2" src="images/SZ_reload.png" />
   <img id="SZO_3" src="images/SZ_score.png" />
  </div>
 </body>
</html>
```

Save the file and then close it. Go back to the My_Work_Files folder and double-click the default.html file.

You should now see the three new images. You may have to scroll down the web page. Again, do not worry about how the images appear on the page. Just ensure you can see the background image from before and the three new images that we just added.

At this stage quite a few people ask me if HTML5 game development is just the same as being a web developer. Yes in the same way an Xbox console developer is just a C#/C++ Forms developer. However HTML5 games do not look and feel like a normal website, do they? As you develop this game you will find out that a HTML5 games developer has to learn everything about being a web developer and then more. You will need to work out where the supposed boundaries lie for a web developer and then learn how far you can push them for your game's engine.

In this chapter we have managed to code our four initial graphical elements on to our screen. They may not look like much to look at as they do not seem to be in the right place nor the right size. However not to worry, as in the next chapter we will apply CSS to the four images which will align them exactly where we want them to be.

CHAPTER 3

Time to Apply a Little CSS

```
#tower-of-pisa
    {
        font-style: italic;
    }
```

CSS, which stands for Cascading Style Sheets, is a language that is used to help style and design web sites. It can be used to describe how the page should look in terms of color, layout, and fonts.

So why do we need this for our game? Previously, we imagined HTML as the skeleton or bone structure of our game. CSS code will be the look and appearance of our game. If you are familiar with building web sites, however, you may be wondering how big a role CSS actually plays in HTML5 game development.

With the arrival of CSS3, animations in CSS allow the browser to determine which elements should get GPU layers, which results in hardware acceleration. Do not start moving all your animations over to CSS en masse, however. It is generally not a good idea to give every element its own layer. If you do, then your GPU will run out memory— quickly. I am sure you will agree that there is no worse feeling as a developer than when you receive the dreaded "Out of Memory" error.

© Zarrar Chishti 2017
Z. Chishti, *Cross Over to HTML5 Game Development*,
https://doi.org/10.1007/978-1-4842-3291-0_3

Start with a Quick Test

Before we align and resize our images, let's start our CSS file with a simple test. The test is to see if we can make the entire background of our page the color red. By doing this, we will make sure that the default.html page is communicating successfully with our CSS page.

Let's open the SZ_master.css file. When the file opens, it should be completely blank. Type the following lines:

```
html {
    height: 100%;
    }
body {
    padding: 0 0 0 0;
    margin: 0;
    user-select: none;
    background-colour: red;
}
```

You can now save and close this file.

As you can see from this code, the syntax of a CSS file consists of three parts.

- selector

  This is usually the HTML <tag> that you want to define. In the preceding code, we defined the <html> and <body> tags as selectors.

- property

  As the name suggests, here we define what property of the tag we wish to apply a style to. In our <html> example, we defined the height property to style.

- value

  The actual style that you wish to define for the property. In our case, we decided that the height of our <html> tag is 100% of the screen size.

Interestingly, you can specify the same parameters for multiple tags by simply grouping them.

Before testing, we need to link this file into our default.html file. Reopen the default.html file and type the following new (in bold) line:

```
<html>
 <head>
  <link href="css/SZ_master.css" rel="stylesheet" />
 </head>
 <body>
  <div id="SZ_maincontent">
   <img id="SZO_0" src="images/SZ_background_image.jpg" />
   <img id="SZO_1" src="images/SZ_gun.png" />
   <img id="SZO_2" src="images/SZ_reload.png" />
   <img id="SZO_3" src="images/SZ_score.png" />
  </div>
 </body>
</html>
```

Save the file and then close it. Go back to the My_Work_Files folder and double-click the default.html file.

You should see the same screen as last time (i.e., the four images) but with a red background instead of white. This is good because it means that you successfully linked the CSS file to the main HTML page.

We have covered quite a lot of CSS techniques in the SZ_master.css file. Let's go through them.

- html {height: 100%; }

   This sets the height of our HTML page to 100%. It means that our content should be able to cover the visible screen from the top to the bottom.

It is worth noting that we can use the properties *min-height* and *max-height* to override the height property.

- padding: 0 0 0 0;

   This clears an area around the content of the page. Think of making a four-sided margin where you specify how thick you want it to be. In our case, we want the content to cover the entire page, so we set the padding for all four sides to 0. The four 0's correspond to top, right, bottom, left.

- position: fixed;

   As the name suggests, this positions the image to a fixed location based on the browser window. So top: 0; means 0 pixels (*pixels* is a measurement) from the top of the browser (i.e., you want it fixed to the top). Similarly, bottom: 0; means that you want the image placed at the bottom of the browser window. Finally, left: 0; and right: 0; refer to the image placed to the left or the right of the browser window.

- `margin:0;`

  The margin sets the size of the white space around the element. In our case, we do not want any white space around the edges of the screen.

- `user-select: none;` We can control how our player interacts with the text elements on the screen by using the `user-select` property. In this case, it is set to `none`, which means that we do not want the user to select or click any text elements. The reason for this is that it may distract from playing the actual game (for example, text that allows the user to select the high score).

- `background-colour: red;` As the name suggests, this sets the background color of the screen. If you wish, try to replace the word `red` with `yellow` or any color of your choice. Save the file and refresh the browser.

We also added another line of code to our HTML file:

```
<link href="css/SZ_master.css" rel="stylesheet" />
```

The `link` tag is the standard way to include a CSS file on the page. The `href` specifies the location of the CSS file that we wish to include. The `rel` tag specifies the relationship between the HTML file and the CSS file. In this case, the CSS file acts as a style sheet for the HTML file.

Our Background Image

Let's start fixing the images. We will start with the background image. Ideally, we want this image to fill our page (much like the red background color did).

Open the SZ_master.css file and type the following new lines(all new text is in bold):

```
html {
     height: 100%;
   }
body {
     padding: 0 0 0 0;
     margin: 0;
     user-select: none;
   }
img  {
     max-width: 100%;
     height: auto;
     user-drag: none;
     user-select: none;
     -moz-user-select: none;
     -webkit-user-drag: none;
     -webkit-user-select: none;
     -ms-user-select: none;
   }
#SZ0_0 {
     position: fixed;
     top: 0;
     left: 0;
     min-width: 100%;
     min-height: 100%;
   }
```

Save the file and then close it. Go back to the My_Work_Files folder and double-click the default.html file.

Note that we have removed the background-colour: red; from body tag. Ensure that you remove that line from your code. Your file should look exactly like what is shown.

You may be wondering why we have coded the user-select property in four different ways. The first method is the standard property in CSS (i.e., user-select). We then go on to define the vendor-prefixed properties offered by the various rendering engines. This allows properties to be set specific to each individual browser engine to safely account for inconsistencies between implementations.

The following are the vendor-prefixed properties that we used:

- webkit for Chrome and Safari

- moz for Firefox

- ms for Internet Explorer

Historically, we used these prefixes to implement new CSS features prior to final clarification by the W3. Therefore, over time, the prefixes will be removed for the final version of the property.

Save the file and then close it. Go back to the My_Work_Files folder and double-click the default.html file.

Your screen should look the following screenshot.

You should first notice the background image now covers the entire screen. Also, the other three images are completely gone from the screen. Not to worry. They are still there— behind the background image.

Further Information

The first style added to our CSS was for the <img> tag. This means that the styles defined apply to every image that we add to our page. I am sure you will agree that this is a big time-saving technique, because the alternative is to repeat the styles laboriously for every image that we add.

Anyhow, not every image requires the same styles. You can see the second style is specifically written for one of the image tags, which is identified as #SZO_0.

The styles that we put in the <img> tag are the more generic styles that should apply to all images. We can then add an individual style to a specific image and add more styles. We can even override styles that were written in the <img> tag.

Before we leave this, why did we call the tag #SZ0_0? If you go back to Section 2.3, notice the following:

```
<img id="SZ0_0" src="images/SZ_background_image.jpg" />
```

This image is identified as SZ0_0. In CSS, you can identify the image by placing the hash sign (#) before the ID.

Let's take a look at the new CSS techniques that we used.

- max-width: 100%; height: auto;

  We want the images to stretch to the full width of their container. Also, we want the code to automatically determine what the height should be when the new width is applied. This ensures that we keep the aspect ratio of the image when resizing.

- user-drag: none;

  We do not want the user to be able to drag the images on the screen.

- -moz, -webkit and -ms

  These are CSS extensions, which are properties that web browsers support but are not (yet) part of the official CSS specification.

- top: 0; left: 0;

  Sets the top and left edge of the image. In this case, we want the image to always position itself in the top-left corner of its container.

- min-width: 100%; min-height: 100%;

  As it suggests, we want the image's minimum width and height to be the full size of its container.

Our Other Images

We can start fixing the other three images. First, here's a reminder about the images and where they should go:

- SZ_gun

  The gun image should reside in the bottom-right corner of the screen.

- SZ_reload

  The Reload button should appear in the top-left corner of the screen.

- SZ_score

  The score image should appear in the top-right corner of the screen.

Now open the SZ_master.css file and type the following new lines (all new text is in bold):

```
html {
     height: 100%;
     }
body {
     padding: 0 0 0 0;
     margin: 0;
     user-select: none;
     }
img  {
     max-width: 100%;
     height: auto;
     user-drag: none;
     user-select: none;
```

```css
        -moz-user-select: none;
        -webkit-user-drag: none;
        -webkit-user-select: none;
        -ms-user-select: none;
    }
#SZo_0 {
        position: fixed;
        top: 0;
        left: 0;
        min-width: 100%;
        min-height: 100%;
    }
 #SZo_1 {
        position: fixed;
        bottom: 0;
        right: 0;
}
 #SZo_2 {
        position: fixed;
        top: 0;
        left: 0;
}
 #SZo_3 {
        position: fixed;
        top: 0;
        right: 0;
}
```

Save the file and then close it.

33

In this code, we have defined three properties for each of the three images. However, notice that the properties and their subsequent values are exactly the same. Earlier, I touched on the fact that we can specify the same parameters for multiple tags by simply grouping them. So if you wish, you can try that with the preceding code by replacing the bold code with the following:

```
#SZO_1, #SZO_2, #SZO_3 {
        position: fixed;
        top: 0;
        right: 0;
}
```

Go back to the My_Work_Files folder and double-click the default. html file.

Your screen should look like the following screenshot.

Although you can now see all four images in their aligned positions, they aren't quite the right size; however, do not worry about that. In the next chapter, we will use JavaScript to resize the images.

Further Information

The position property specifies the type of positioning method used for an element (static, relative, fixed, or absolute). Elements are then positioned using the top, right, bottom, and left properties. However, these properties will not work unless the position property is set first. They also work differently, depending on the position value.

Let's take a brief look at the four position values.

- static elements are not affected by the top, right, bottom, left properties.

- relative means setting the top, right, bottom, and left properties of a relatively positioned element causes it to be adjusted away from its normal position.

- fixed means positioned relative to the viewport, which means it always stays in the same place even if the page is scrolled. The top, right, bottom, and left properties are used to position the element.

- absolute means positioned relative to the nearest ancestor (instead of positioned relative to the viewport, like fixed).

In our case, we used fixed along with bottom: 0; right: 0;. In the previous section, we set the image's top-left corner; whereas here we can set the image from the bottom-right corner of its container.

Since we need our gun to always be positioned in the bottom-right corner of the screen, it makes more sense in this case to use the bottom-right property rather than the top-left property.

CHAPTER 4

Apply Intelligence with JavaScript

"Always code as if the guy who ends up maintaining your code will be a violent psychopath who knows where you live."

Rick Osborne

As you have learned, HTML is the bone structure and CSS is the look and appearance of our game. So what does JavaScript bring to the table? JavaScript is a programming language used for creating interactivity in web sites. So we could say that we use JavaScript as the master controller of our game.

So why do we need it for our game? The obvious answer is that the game needs to be able to create the zombies, fire the gun, and respond to user commands. This is true, but there is a huge amount of other work that the game needs JavaScript to perform. For example, in the previous chapter, we discovered a need to resize our images based on the browser size. Let's do that now using JavaScript.

Why Do We Need to Resize?

Our game will be playable on many types of devices; computer PCs, laptops, mobile devices, tablets and even consoles linked to massive TVs. Within each of these devices, there are many different screen sizes. Mobile phones and laptops come in a wide range of screen sizes.

37

© Zarrar Chishti 2017
Z. Chishti, *Cross Over to HTML5 Game Development*,
https://doi.org/10.1007/978-1-4842-3291-0_4

Let's go one step further. What if someone resizes their Internet browser window? Now we are talking an infinite number of combinations.

Creating graphics for everything conceivable would be extremely time-consuming. Actually, it would be impossible because it seems there is always a new model of phone (therefore, a new screen size) or a new computer monitor coming out. So we need to find a universal way to resize the images for any screen size.

How Do We Universally Resize?

If you have a 30cm ruler handy, take a look at it. Imagine we design our game for the 15cm mark. We can use JavaScript to tell us what the actual size is on the ruler. So let's say that it comes back as 10cm. We can then work out a ratio (i.e., 10 divided by 15) that can be used against all measurements; 10 divided by 15 is 0.67. This means when we apply this to our images, they will be made smaller, which is what we want. Similarly, if the size came back bigger, let's say 20cm, the ratio would reflect this and make all images bigger than we had designed them.

Let's write a function to work out this ratio. Open SZ_main.js. This file should be completely blank. Type the following lines:

```
//global vars
  //need to store the ratio
    var ratio;
  //need easy access to the width
    var newWidth;
//function that gets called when game starts
$(window).load(function () {
    //need to grab an instance of our screen
    var div = $(window);
    //we can now work out the ratio
    ratio = (div.width() / 1024);
```

```
 //while we are here we can grab the width for future use
 newWidth = div.width();
});
```

You can now save and close this file.

Definitions for the various JavaScript terms can be found in the Further Information section below. One other thing to note is that I have tried to enter as many comments for explanations as we have lines of code (as you are accustomed to in your own programming language).

Before we can test, we need to link this file to our default.html file. So, let's reopen default.html and type the following three new lines (all the new text is in bold):

```
<html>
 <head>
  <script src="js/jquery.js"></script>
  <script src="js/jquery-ui.js"></script>
  <script src="js/SZ_main.js"></script>
  <link href="css/SZ_master.css" rel="stylesheet" />
 </head>
 <body>
  <div id="SZ_maincontent">
   <img id="SZO_0" src="images/SZ_background_image.jpg" />
   <img id="SZO_1" src="images/SZ_gun.png" />
   <img id="SZO_2" src="images/SZ_reload.png" />
   <img id="SZO_3" src="images/SZ_score.png" />
  </div>
 </body>
</html>
```

Save the file and then close it.

These three new lines involve the <script> tag. In our case, we chose to link this tag to an external script file through the src attribute. Alternatively, we could have used the same tag to define a client-side script containing scripting statements.

Now double-click the default.html file.

Nothing has changed, has it? This is due to the JavaScript code working on background tasks. Also, we have not yet told it to do anything to our images. All we did was store a value in the code (i.e., the ratio).

All the same, it would be nice to see if our first bit of code is working. Let's add a line of code that will show a message box on our screen. In this box, we will put the value that our code has just worked out for the ratio. This is not terribly exciting but at least we get some form of feedback from our code. Now that is exciting.

Now open the SZ_main.js file and type the following new lines (those that are in bold):

```
//global vars
  //need to store the ratio
    var ratio;
  //need easy access to the width
    var newWidth;
//function that gets called when game starts
$(window).load(function () {
    //need to grab an instance of our screen
    var div = $(window);
    //we can now work out the ratio
    ratio = (div.width() / 1024);
    //while we are here we can grab the width for future use
    newWidth = div.width();
  //We are adding in a temporary bit of code here
  window.alert("Hi this is your code and I have just worked out
  that the ratio will be "+ratio);
});
```

We can now save and close this file.

We just used the `window.alert()` method, which typically displays an alert box with a specified message and an OK button. Normally, alert boxes are used to make sure that important information is displayed to our users. In our case, we used the alert box to inform us of the value of a variable, which at this point in our coding, we do not have access to.

I should note that alert boxes take the focus away from the current window by forcing the browser to read the message. I would not recommend overusing this method, as it removes the user's focus from playing the game until the box is closed.

Go back to our `My_Work_Files` folder and double-click the `default.html` file. You should see our web site with a message box:

What we have here is our code talking to us. It is telling us the value it worked out for the ratio.

Before we go on, we need to remove the two lines that we just added. Open the SZ_main.js file. After you remove the two lines, the code should look like this again:

```
//global vars
  //need to store the ratio
    var ratio;
  //need easy access to the width
    var newWidth;
//function that gets called when game starts
$(window).load(function () {
    //need to grab an instance of our screen
    var div = $(window);
    //we can now work out the ratio
    ratio = (div.width() / 1024);
    //while we are here we can grab the width for future use
    newWidth = div.width();
});
```

You will create many wonderful functions in this book, and no doubt in the games that you go on to develop. However, I hope you treasure this moment as I did back in 1994 when I was learning to code Pascal.

Did the window box not appear? Not to worry. One of these tips should help:

- Go back and recheck that every line of code is the same

- Did you miss any semicolons (;) at the end of your lines?

- Did you make sure that you added the three lines of code in the HTML file?

- Are all nine files in the js folder as they should be?

If your code is still not working, then please do not hesitate to message me on Twitter @zarrarchishti.

Next, we will put this ratio to work.

Further Information

What is a function?

We will write a lot of functions in JavaScript. A *function* is simply a set of instructions that are executed when the function itself is called to run. So when our function is called, it determines the ratio and stores the width of the screen.

Why are lines starting with // written like conversational English?

When you start the line with double forward slashes (//), you are telling the computer to ignore this line. Why would you do that? Well, it is there for us and it is called a *comment line*. Its purpose is to leave messages for ourselves (or other programmers). By leaving messages, we break up the code and make the whole program easier to read. You can write anything you like. I like to use it to explain why the code after the comment was originally written.

You do not have to comment every line; however, I was always taught to comment as many lines as I code. This may appear overkill to some programmers; however, I have found that when I return to my code after a few years, the comments I wrote help me understand the reasoning behind the code.

Why did we add the other two files to our HTML file?

When it came to adding the SZ_main.js file, we also added jQuery and jQuery-UI files. These are essentially filled with advanced functions (like the one you wrote). As long as we use their functions, all we have to do is add them to our HTML.

These functions are fast, reliable, and rich with features. Some of the biggest companies in the world use them, as do small game developers like us.

Let's now look at some of the JavaScript code we wrote.

- `var ratio;`

  We are declaring a variable here called ratio. A *variable* is a container that can store data. We can put data into ratio and read from it.

- `$(window).load(function () {`

  This function is called once the entire page has loaded. This makes it extremely useful, because the instructions inside this function require the elements (for instance, the images) to be present and loaded on the screen.

- `var div = $(window);`

  As we discovered before, the var creates a container to store data. However, in this case, we are using it to pass an instance of the entire window. This variable called div now contains all the important information concerning our window. For example, we go on to use the following statement.

- `newWidth = div.width();`

  This means we can store the window's width in our variable called newWidth.

Let's Resize Our Images

As a reminder, these are the images with their ideal sizes:

- SZ_gunWidth 133px and Height 150px

- SZ_reloadWidth 200px and Height 90px

- SZ_scoreWidth 235px and Height 100px

Open the SZ_setupContent.js file in the js folder. When the file opens, it should be completely blank. Type the following lines:

```
//main function
  function main_call_setupContent() {
  //need to resize all elements
  //first we set their normal sizes in CSS

  //Gun
  $('#SZO_1').css('width', 150 * ratio);
  $('#SZO_1').css('height', 150 * ratio);

  //Reload Button
  $('#SZO_2').css('width', 200 * ratio);
  $('#SZO_2').css('height', 90 * ratio);

  //Score
  $('#SZO_3').css('width', 235 * ratio);
  $('#SZO_3').css('height', 100 * ratio);

}
```

Save and close this file.

At some point, you may wish to revisit this function and recode the flow. I recommend that you place the values of the image IDs into an array; for example,

```
var image_ids= ["#SZO_1","#SZO_2","#SZO_3"];
```

You would then also need to place the values for each image into another array; for example,

```
var image_sizes = [ [150, 150], [200, 90], [235, 100] ];
```

You could then code a for loop to execute the same code three times, substituting the ID with the next value in the ID array, and substituting the width and height values with the values in the size array.

Open the SZ_main.js file and type the following new lines (the new text is in bold):

```
//global vars
  //need to store the ratio
    var ratio;
  //need easy access to the width
    var newWidth;
//function that gets called when game starts
$(window).load(function () {
    //need to grab an instance of our screen
    var div = $(window);
    //we can now work out the ratio
    ratio = (div.width() / 1024);
    //while we are here we can grab the width for future use
    newWidth = div.width();

    //let's apply the ratio to our elements
    main_call_setupContent();
});
```

Before we can test, we need to link this file to our default.html file. Reopen the default.html file and type the following line (the new text is in bold):

```
<html>
 <head>
  <script src="js/jquery.js"></script>
  <script src="js/jquery-ui.js"></script>
  <script src="js/SZ_main.js"></script>
  <script src="js/SZ_setupContent.js"></script>
  <link href="css/SZ_master.css" rel="stylesheet" />
 </head>
 <body>
  <div id="SZ_maincontent">
   <img id="SZO_0" src="images/SZ_background_image.jpg" />
   <img id="SZO_1" src="images/SZ_gun.png" />
   <img id="SZO_2" src="images/SZ_reload.png" />
   <img id="SZO_3" src="images/SZ_score.png" />
  </div>
 </body>
</html>
```

Go back to the My_Work_Files folder and double-click the default. html file. You should now see the three elements resized, as shown in the following screenshot:

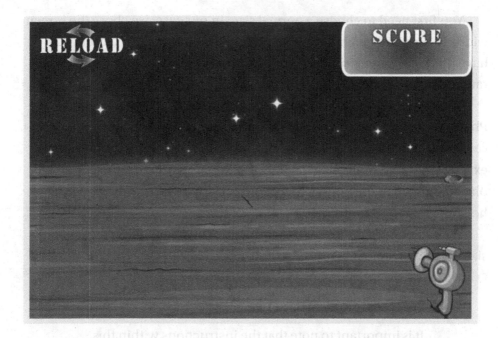

Congratulations! We have now finished the first part of the game! We will now develop the game further in the coming chapters. However, the main building blocks are done. From this point forward, we will be adding more HTML, more CSS, and yes, even more JavaScript until our game is finally playable.

Where did the ideal sizes come from (for example, the gun: Width 175px and Height 200px)?

The step that is taken before any development can start is the layout design of each screen. This is where you physically place the elements, like the gun, on a screen.

You first need to choose a normal size. In our case, we chose the screen width 1025px and height 800px. Of course, the chances that a user will have this exact screen size are very slim. This is why we worked out the ratio earlier.

You can use any software design program, such as Macromedia Photoshop or Fireworks, to create layout files. Once we create our new canvas size of 1024 × 800, we can then resize and reposition our elements exactly where we would like them on the canvas. So, for example, we placed our gun in the bottom-right corner, with a 175px width and a 200px height.

We can now apply our ratio to the width and height to get an accurate size for the screen being used.

We created a function in JavaScript as follows:

- ```
  function main_call_setupContent() {
  ```

  It is important to note that the instructions within this function are not executed until we call this function, which we do in SZ_main.js by calling main_call_ setupContent();.

- ```
  main_call_setupContent();
  ```

  Only now are the instructions executed by the program.

Finally, let's take a look at the following line of code:

- ```
  $('#SZ0_1').css('width', 150 * ratio);
  ```

  We can manipulate an element's CSS directly from the JavaScript. This is an extremely powerful and useful tool in game development. For instance, if we want an element to become bigger after shooting it, we can do this directly from the JavaScript code that was used to identify the button click.
  ```

CHAPTER 5

Take a Shot: Part 1

"Code never lies, comments sometimes do."

Ron Jeffries

In this chapter, we'll work on what we want our gun to do. When the user presses anywhere on the screen, apart from the Reload button, it should be treated as a shot. How a shot happens and the consequences of a shot are dealt with in Chapter 7. For now, let's look at reacting to a user click.

There will be a few awesome techniques employed, including sprite sheets for animation and mathematics for fluid movement. As you build other games in the future, you may find yourself coming back and reusing these functions and techniques. This is exactly what happens in commercial game development.

Incidentally, some of the code in this chapter is from a project I did recently for a children's game that is hosted in the Kelvingrove Art Gallery and Museum in Glasgow.

Changing Our Cursor and Registering a Click

Normal Cursor   Crosshair Cursor

In shooting games like the one we are developing, the mouse cursor typically becomes a crosshair.

51

Changing the cursor can be done simply using CSS. Open the SZ_ master.css file in our CSS folder. Type the following new line (in bold):

```
html {
      height: 100%;
      }

+
body {
        padding: 0 0 0 0;
        margin: 0;
        user-select: none;
        cursor: crosshair;
      }
img   {
        max-width: 100%;
        height: auto;
        user-drag: none;
        user-select: none;
        -moz-user-select: none;
        -webkit-user-drag: none;
        -webkit-user-select: none;
        -ms-user-select: none;
      }
#SZO_0 {
        position: fixed;
        top: 0;
        left: 0;
        min-width: 100%;
        min-height: 100%;
      }
```

```
#SZO_1 {
        position: fixed;
        bottom: 0;
        right: 0;
}
#SZO_2 {
        position: fixed;
        top: 0;
        left: 0;
}
#SZO_3 {
        position: fixed;
        top: 0;
        right: 0;
}
```

Save the file and then close it. Go back to our My_Work_Files folder and double-click the default.html file.

Notice that the mouse cursor has changed from an arrow to crosshairs.

So what is the line that we just wrote?

cursor: crosshair; specifies the type of cursor to be displayed when pointing with a mouse.

You may be curious as to what other types of cursors are available to you. The following is a list of cursor types. If you wish, replace the word *crosshair* in the CSS file with any of these words.

53

- e-resize
- move
- nw-resize
- s-resize
- text
- no-drop
- grab
- n-resize
- pointer
- se-resize
- w-resize
- not-allowed
- help
- ne-resize
- progress
- sw-resize
- wait

Making Our Gun Act More Realistic

The more engaging the gameplay is for users, the more they will enjoy playing it over and over again. One of the ways to increase user engagement is with the small details that we can add to our game. For instance, wouldn't it be nice if the gun reacted when the user moved the cursor across the screen?

To do this, we will use JavaScript. Open the SZ_movement.js file in the js folder. When the file opens, it should be completely blank. Type the following lines:

```
function rotateGun(e) {
//using the e value we can deduce the X co-ordinates
var xPos = e.clientX;

//We need to work out where the mouse cursor is as a percentage
of the width of the screen

//We will work this out by dividing the current X position
by the overall screen width which if you remember we put in
newWidth
var currentXPositionPercentage = xPos/newWidth;

//We now want to apply this to the maximum amount of rotation
which is 50 however the starting rotation is -15 not 0
var amountToRotate = -15 + (currentXPositionPercentage * 50);

//Let's rotate the gun!
  $("#SZ0_1").css('transform', 'rotate('+amountToRotate+'deg)');
}
```

We can now save and close this file.

A detailed explanation of this code is in the following "Further Information" section.

Before we can test, we need to link this file to our `default.html` file. Reopen the `default.html` file and type the following new line along with the extra bit of text in one of our existing lines (all new text is in bold):

```
<html>
 <head>
  <script src="js/jquery.js"></script>
  <script src="js/jquery-ui.js"></script>
  <script src="js/SZ_main.js"></script>
  <script src="js/SZ_setupContent.js"></script>
  <script src="js/SZ_movement.js"></script>
  <link href="css/SZ_master.css" rel="stylesheet" />
 </head>
 <body>
  <div id="SZ_maincontent">
   <img id="SZO_0" onmousemove="rotateGun(event)" src="images/
   SZ_background_image.jpg" />
   <img id="SZO_1" src="images/SZ_gun.png" />
   <img id="SZO_2" src="images/SZ_reload.png" />
   <img id="SZO_3" src="images/SZ_score.png" />
  </div>
 </body>
</html>
```

Save the file and then close it. Now double-click the `default.html` file.

Try moving the mouse along the screen. The gun should rotate as if looking to aim at the target we are looking to shoot at. I am sure you will agree that this is far more engaging than a static gun.

I want to discuss an interesting point about something in the preceding code. onmousemove, as the name suggests, triggers a JavaScript function when the user moves the mouse over the image. It does not trigger on touchscreen devices such as mobile phones. You may wish to revisit this portion of code in the future and modify it so that it triggers when the user touches any part of the image.

Next, we will look at making the gun fire!

Did the code not work? One of the new lines is different from the usual way we add code. Let's go through this together:

Open the default.html file.

Locate the line that starts with

```
<img id="SZ0_0" onmousemove="rotateGun(event)"
src="images/SZ_background_image.jpg" />
```

Have you added the extra bit of text exactly as it's shown?

Add the following text:

```
onmousemove="rotateGun(event)"
```

between

```
id="SZ0_0" and src="
```

If your code is still not working, then please do not hesitate to message me on Twitter @zarrarchishti.

We wrote the following line in JavaScript:

```
var xPos = e.clientX;
```

the e was passed to our function as follows:

```
function rotateGun(e) {
```

The e contains all the information from an event that has occurred. In this instance, it is a mouse movement on our image, which we declared as follows:

```
<img id="SZ0_0" onmousemove="rotateGun(event)"
src="images/SZ_background_image.jpg" />
```

When the user moves the mouse over this image, our `rotateGun` function is called and the data from the movement is passed in.

In the first line, you see that we extract the "clientX" from e. This is the horizontal coordinate (more commonly referred to as the *x axis*) of the mouse event that has just occurred.

So what is this X-axis? Try to imagine the left-to-right user action of your screen as the X axis. The following image illustrates the relationship we want with the X-axis and the gun's rotation.

The maximum rotation between the far left and the far right gun is 50 degrees. So by finding out exactly where we are on the screen, we can use a mathematical equation to determine what the exact rotation of the gun should be.

One further point: the code we use to actually rotate the gun is done by using both JavaScript and CSS. The JavaScript does most of the work here by namely doing the following:

- Alerts a function every time the user moves the mouse

- Determines how much of the mouse has moved

- Applies the value above to our mathematical equation

From here, we hand this value over to CSS, which then actually rotates the gun.

Feel free to play with the numbers and test the different rotations that occur; for example, change the following line

```
var amountToRotate = -15 + (currentXPositionPercentage * 50);
```

Change the 50 to 100. You will notice a far bigger change in how the gun moves. Keep changing the number until you reach a level of rotation that you are happy with. If you want to go back, simple type the preceding code.

Finally, we come across another example of manipulating CSS in JavaScript in the following line:

```
$("#SZ0_1").css('transform', 'rotate('+amountToRotate+'deg)');
```

As the word indicates, the `transform` property applies a transformation to any element. Other transformations include `scale`, `move`, and `skew`.

Animating the Gun with Sprite Sheets

When the user clicks the screen, we want to make our gun fire. To do this, we will work with something called *sprite sheets*. Before we can start adding our sprite sheets, we need to write some code. This is because a sprite sheet is not something your browser (e.g., Chrome) can process by itself like it does with the images we have used so far.

We need to write some code that instructs the browser on how to handle our sprite sheet images. To do this, we will use JavaScript. As a word of caution, the code is slightly lengthier than what you have written so far. I encourage you to persevere since this particular function can be reused in every project that you do, without changing anything in the code. Please ensure that you copy all the code exactly as shown.

Part 1

Open the `SZ_SS.js` file in your `js` folder. When the file opens, it should be completely blank. Type the following lines:

```
//We need a one stop function that will allow us to process
sprite sheets
function setup_SpriteSheet(div_name, image_name, no_of_frames,
widthx, heightx) {
```

```
//need the ratio of the container's width/height
  var imageOrgRatio = $(div_name).height() / $(div_name).
  width() ;

//need to ensure no trailing decimals
  var ratio2 = Math.round(ratio * 10) / 10;

//check that the width is completely divisible by the no of
frames
  var newDivisible = Math.round((widthx * ratio2) / no_of_
frames);

//the new width will be the number of frames multiplied by our
new divisible
  var newWidthx = newDivisible * no_of_frames;

//also the new height will be our ratio times the height of
the div containing our image
  var newHeightx = heightx * ratio2;
//apply our new width to our CSS
  $(div_name).css('width', (newWidthx));

//apply our new height to our CSS
  $(div_name).css('height', newHeightx);
//
//take the image name and apply as a background image to our div
  $(div_name).css('background-image', 'url(' + image_name + ')');

//finally we need to apply a background size remembering we
need to multiply width by the number of frames
  $(div_name).css('background-size', newWidthx * no_of_frames
  + 'px ' + newHeightx + 'px');
}
```

Initially, I was tempted to just add a standard sprite sheet library; however, by coding it ourselves, we have more flexibility in future games. As you build more games, you discover that not all sprite sheets—or all parameters for using them—are the same. Therefore, you will need to revisit the preceding function and tweak it to make sure that it fits your current project. If we had only used a standard function, it would have severely limited the types of sprite sheets that you could use.

As with all the other standard functions, as long as we link this file to any HTML file in the future, our little function can be used.

Further Information

What are sprite sheets?

A sprite sheet is a special image that contains several images in a tiled grid arrangement.

So why use sprite sheets?

Sprite sheets allow games to run faster, and more importantly, to take up less memory. By compiling several graphics into a single file, you enable your game to use the graphics while only needing to load a single file.

How are sprite sheets designed?

There are three parts to our sprite sheet. First, the normal static state is when the gun reloads and when the gun fires. The following illustrates this:

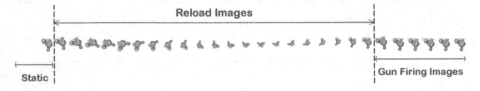

Why did we need to write our own special function to use sprite sheets?

There are many ways to deal with sprite sheets. Each programmer designs their code to manipulate the sprite sheet that suits them. I have used a very simple method here, which deals with sprites that have been laid out linearly.

Also, our game does not require sophisticated use of any sprite sheets. As you are writing all the code, I wanted to make sure that you only had to write the minimum amount necessary. However, you can use this code as a basis for your next game and build on it as you see necessary.

Part 2

Now that we have set up our function to handle any sprite sheets, we can test it with our gun. First, we need to replace the static image for our gun with the sprite sheet version.

Go to the images folder in the Raw Images folder of the My_Work_Files folder. Copy the file named SZ_gun_SS.png to the Images folder, which should now look like the following screenshot.

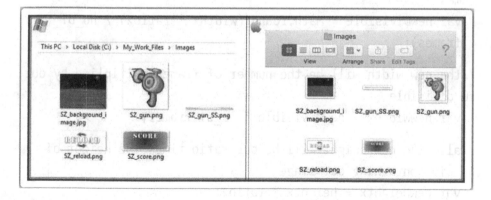

Part 3

Next, we need to inform the code that the gun is a sprite sheet and pass all the information about it (e.g., the image name that you copied).

We will use JavaScript to do this. Reopen the SZ_SS.js file in the js folder. Type the following new lines (all new text is in bold):

```
//We need a one stop function that will allow us to process
sprite sheets
function setup_SpriteSheet(div_name, image_name, no_of_frames,
widthx, heightx) {

  //need the ratio of the container's width/height
    var imageOrgRatio =  $(div_name).height() / $(div_name).
    width() ;

  //need to ensure no trailing decimals
    var ratio2 = Math.round(ratio * 10) / 10;

  //check that the width is completely divisible by the no of
frames
    var newDivisible = Math.round((widthx * ratio2) / no_of_
    frames);

  //the new width will be the number of frames multiplied by our
new divisible
    var newWidthx = newDivisible * no_of_frames;

  //also the new height will be our ratio times the height of
the div containing our image
    var newHeightx = heightx * ratio2;

  //apply our new width to our CSS
    $(div_name).css('width', (newWidthx));

  //apply our new height to our CSS
```

```
    $(div_name).css('height', newHeightx);
//
  //take the image name and apply as a background image to our div
    $(div_name).css('background-image', 'url(' + image_name + ')');

  //finally we need to apply a background size remembering we
need to multiply width by the no of frames
    $(div_name).css('background-size', newWidthx * no_of_frames
    + 'px ' + newHeightx + 'px');
}

//setup the Gun
function setup_gun_SS(){
 //first let's setup our gun SS
    setup_SpriteSheet("#SZ0_1","Images/SZ_gun_SS.png",28,150,150);
 //need to access a special function in our js/ss.js file
    $("#SZ0_1").animateSprite({
        fps: 10,
        animations: {
            static: [0],
            reload: [1,2,3,4,5,6,7,8,9,10,11,12,13,14,15,16,17,
            18,19,20,21,22,23],
            fire: [24,25,26,27,28],
        },
        duration: 50,
        loop: false,
        complete: function () {
            // use complete only when you set animations with
            'loop: false'
            //alert("animation End");
        }
    });
}
```

Save and close the file.

It can get quite tedious to write in all the different frames needed for a particular animation. Imagine if you had over 500 frames! In the future, when revisiting the animateSprite function, change it to take a range of values. You could also try to code the function to take a set of ranges; for example, frames (1 to 7, 9 to 11, and 29 to 31).

Before we can test, we need to make the following two changes to our HTML file:

- Reference new JavaScript files in the head

- Enclose the images inside their own divs

Reopen the default.html file and type the following new lines. Please be careful to replace the existing lines of code so that the entire file looks like the following code (all new text is in bold):

```
<html>
 <head>
  <script src="js/jquery.js"></script>
  <script src="js/jquery-ui.js"></script>
  <script src="js/SZ_main.js"></script>
  <script src="js/SZ_setupContent.js"></script>
  <script src="js/SZ_movement.js"></script>
  <script src="js/ss.js"></script>
  <script src="js/SZ_SS.js"></script>
  <link href="css/SZ_master.css" rel="stylesheet" />
 </head>
 <body>
  <div id="SZ_maincontent">
   <img id="SZO_0" src="images/SZ_background_image.
   jpg"  onmousemove="rotateGun(event)"  />
   <div id="SZO_1" ></div>
   <div id="SZO_2" >
```

```
  <img  src="images/SZ_reload.png" />
  </div>
  <div id="SZO_3" >
   <img src="images/SZ_score.png" />
  </div>
 </div>
 </body>
</html>
```

Further Information

In this section, we set up our first sprite sheet with the following code:

setup_SpriteSheet("#SZO_1","Images/SZ_gun_SS.png",28,150,150);

Let's take each parameter in the brackets separately.

- #SZO_1 is the image ID

- Images/SZ_gun_SS.png is the location of the sprite sheet

- 28 is the total number of images contained within our sprite sheet

- 150,150 is the size of each individual image within the sprite sheet

You may have noticed that we applied a special function to our image. Let's take a closer look at each line of this function.

- `fps:`

  The ideal *frames per second* that we would like to apply
  to the sprite sheet animations

- `animations: {`

  We can subdivide the images within a sprite sheet into
  individual animations

- `duration:`

  The length of time that we want to run each animation
  for (in milliseconds)

- `loop:`

  Once the animation finishes, do we want the animation
  to repeat or stop?

- `complete: function () {`

  If the `loop` option is set to false (i.e., no repeat), then
  we can give a set of instructions to execute once the
  animation has completed.

Part 4

Finally, we need to ensure that we are calling the `setup_gun_SS` function.
We can do this in the `SZ_setupContent` file, which initializes all of our
images.

Open the `SZ_setupContent.js` file and type the following new lines
(all new text is in bold).

```
//main function
  function main_call_setupContent() {
  //need to resize all elements
  //first we set their normal sizes in CSS

  //Gun
   $('#SZ0_1').css('width', 150 * ratio);
   $('#SZ0_1').css('height', 150 * ratio);

  //Reload Button
   $('#SZ0_2').css('width', 200 * ratio);
   $('#SZ0_2').css('height', 90 * ratio);

  //Score
   $('#SZ0_3').css('width', 235 * ratio);
   $('#SZ0_3').css('height', 100 * ratio);

  //Any sprite sheets?
   //Our Gun
      setup_gun_SS();
}
```

We are now ready to test! Do not expect much, however, because we are initially telling the code to just show the first image. So let's test this and make sure that our code is working as expected.

Save all the files and then close them. Go back to the My_Work_Files folder and double-click the default.html file. The gun should look exactly the same as before. In fact, the whole screen should look the same. This is good because we have replaced our static image of the gun with a sprite sheet and told it to show the first image.

Next, we look at using the code we have written to animate the gun reloading.

Why does my screen look the same as before?

Well, this is great news. After all that work, I suppose it is natural to expect something to be different. Maybe some of those animations like gun-firing perhaps.

The fact that everything looks normal despite us removing the gun's image and replacing it with our massive sprite sheet image is exactly what we wanted from our code.

The gun is not on the screen anymore.

Since this is a large portion of code, here are suggestions for some typical coding errors that may have happened:

- Go back through each line of code and ensure that it matches with what it is written here in the book.

- Check that you placed the } symbol where indicated.

- Make sure that the SZ_gun_SS.png is in the images folder.

- Make sure that you have included the two new JavaScript files in the head of the HTML file (i.e., ss.js and SZ_SS.js).

The gun does not look right.

Either the gun looks a lot bigger than it should or it looks like a part of the image has been cut off. This means that there is a problem with the way the sprite sheet for the gun has been set up; in particular, the setup_gun_SS() function in the SZ_SS.js file. Please recheck your code and ensure that all the lines of code are exactly as shown.

If your code is still not working, then please do not hesitate to message me on Twitter @zarrarchishti.

Reloading Our Gun

We need to concentrate on two aspects of reloading the gun: cause and effect. The cause comes from the user clicking the reload image on the screen. The effect is the gun animating the appropriate images from the sprite sheet.

Open the SZ_touch.js file in the js folder. When the file opens, it should be completely blank. Type the following lines:

```
//this function is called to reload our gun
function reloadGun(e) {
        //play the reload animation of our SS
        $("#SZo_1").animateSprite("play", "reload");
}
```

Save this file and close it.

When revisiting this project, it would be a good idea to provide options for the reload sequence. I suggest a longer sequence if the gun is empty and a shorter sequence if the gun is not. You would need to define two reload functions and then check the gun's status before calling the reload function. This way, you are rewarding the user for reloading before the gun is empty!

Before we can test, we need to link this file and the function to the
`default.html` file. Reopen the `default.html` file and type the following
new line and an addition to an existing line (all in bold):

```html
<html>
 <head>
  <script src="js/jquery.js"></script>
  <script src="js/jquery-ui.js"></script>
  <script src="js/SZ_main.js"></script>
  <script src="js/SZ_setupContent.js"></script>
  <script src="js/SZ_movement.js"></script>
  <script src="js/ss.js"></script>
  <script src="js/SZ_SS.js"></script>
  <script src="js/SZ_touch.js"></script>
  <link href="css/SZ_master.css" rel="stylesheet" />
 </head>
 <body>
  <div id="SZ_maincontent">
   <img id="SZO_0" src="images/SZ_background_image.jpg"
   onmousemove="rotateGun(event)"  />
   <div id="SZO_1" ></div>
   <div id="SZO_2" >
    <img  src="images/SZ_reload.png"  onmousedown="reloadGun
    (event)" />
   </div>
   <div id="SZO_3" >
    <img src="images/SZ_score.png" />
   </div>
  </div>
 </body>
</html>
```

Save the file and then close it. Go back to the My_Work_Files folder and double-click the default.html file.

When the screen comes up, try to click the Reload button. You should see that the gun animates. This time, click the button a few times before the first animation has finished. It's not smooth, is it? We need to fix this so that the gun does not accept a reload request until the previous one has finished.

Reopen the SZ_touch.js file in the js folder. Type the following new lines (in bold):

```
//this function is called to reload our gun
function reloadGun(e) {
        //play the reload animation of our SS
        $("#SZ0_1").animateSprite("play", "reload");
}
//We need a flag to keep track to avoid repetition of animations
before the first has finished
var canIclick= 0;

//this function is called to reload our gun
function reloadGun(e) {
  //Let's check if we can allow this to occur
    if(canIclick== 0){
      //looks like we can so we better set our flag
        canIclick=1;
        $("#SZ0_1").animateSprite("play", "reload");
    }
}
```

Save this file and close it. Go back to the My_Work_Files folder and double-click the default.html file. Again, click the Reload button a few times before the first animation has finished. The problem has been solved.

However, we now have another issue: the game only accepts the reload request once. We cannot make the gun reload after the first try. This is because we have not reset our flag anywhere in our code. So let's do that now. Reopen the SZ_SS.js file and type the following new lines (in bold):

```
//We need a one stop function that will allow us to process
sprite sheets
function setup_SpriteSheet(div_name, image_name, no_of_frames,
widthx, heightx) {

 //need the ratio of the container's width/height
   var imageOrgRatio =  $(div_name).height() / $(div_name).width();

 //need to ensure no trailing decimals
   var ratio2 = Math.round(ratio * 10) / 10;

 //check that the width is completely divisible by the no of
frames
   var newDivisible = Math.round((widthx * ratio2) / no_of_frames);

 //the new width will be the number of frames multiplied by our
new divisible
   var newWidthx = newDivisible * no_of_frames;

 //also the new height will be our ratio times the height of
the div containing our image
   var newHeightx = heightx * ratio2;

 //apply our new width to our CSS
   $(div_name).css('width', (newWidthx));

 //apply our new height to our CSS
   $(div_name).css('height', newHeightx);
 //
 //take the image name and apply as a background image to our div
   $(div_name).css('background-image', 'url(' + image_name + ')');
```

```
    //finally we need to apply a background size remembering we
need to multiply width by the no of frames
    $(div_name).css('background-size', newWidthx * no_of_frames
    + 'px ' + newHeightx + 'px');
}

//setup the Gun
function setup_gun_SS(){
 //first let's setup our gun SS
    setup_SpriteSheet("#SZ0_1","Images/SZ_gun_
SS.png",28,150,150);
 //need to access a special function in our js/ss.js file
    $("#SZ0_1").animateSprite({
        fps: 10,
        animations: {
            static: [0],
            reload: [1,2,3,4,5,6,7,8,9,10,11,12,13,14,15,16,17,
            18,19,20,21,22,23],
            fire: [24,25,26,27,28],
        },
        duration: 50,
        loop: false,
        complete: function () {
            // use complete only when you set animations with
            'loop: false'
            //alert("animation End");
            //we need to reset our universal flag
              canIclick=0;
        }
    });
}
```

Save this file and close it.

When revisiting this project, it would be a good idea to store all of our global vars in a separate file. I am sure that you practice this in your own programming environment; it ensures that your project is manageable in future. If you do create a global var file, make sure to link it in your HTML file using the <script> tag.

Go back to the My_Work_Files folder and double-click the default.html file.

Again, click the Reload button after the first animation has finished. The problem should now be solved.

Next, we will complete this chapter by making our gun fire.

Why did the gun stop reloading after the first try?

Before we tell our code to run the reload command, we ask it if our flag (i.e. canIclick) is set to 0. We initialize canIclick to 0 when the program starts. Once it passes this test, the first thing the code does is set canIclick to 1.

The next time you press the Reload button, it comes back negative—to when asked if canIclick is 0. So ideally, we want to reset canIclick back to 0 once the animation for reloading the gun completes. We do this in a special subfunction of the animate command. This function specifically asks if there are any special instructions to be executed once the animation finishes.

Recall when we discussed the onmousemove event, in which we used the following:

```
<img  src="images/SZ_reload.
png"  onmousedown="reloadGun(event)" /> -
```

As its name suggests, this calls the reloadGun function every time the image is clicked. The following is a shortened list of the event functions that we can use.

- onmouseenter

  This event occurs when the mouse is moved onto an element.

- onmouseleave

  This event occurs when the mouse is moved out of an element.

- onmouseover

  This event occurs when the mouse is moved onto an element or onto one of its children.

- onmouseout

  This event occurs when a user moves the mouse pointer out of an element or out of one of its children.

- onmouseup

  This event occurs when a user releases a mouse button over an element.

Firing Our Gun

As you may expect, the method of making our gun fire is very similar to how we made the gun reload. First, we need to register the user requesting the gun to fire. Then, we need to make the gun animate.

Reopen the SZ_touch.js file in the js folder. Type the following new lines (in bold):

```
//We need a flag to keep track to avoid repetition of animations
before the first has finished
var canIclick= 0;

//this function is called to reload our gun
function reloadGun(e) {
 //Let's check if we can allow this to occur
   if(canIclick== 0){
     //looks like we can so we better set our flag
       canIclick=1;
       $("#SZ0_1").animateSprite("play", "reload");
     }
}

//this function is called to fire our gun
function fireGun(e) {
 //Let's check if we can allow this to occur
   if(canIclick== 0){
     //looks like we can so we better set our flag
       canIclick=1;
       $("#SZ0_1").animateSprite("play", "fire");
     }
}
```

Save the file and close it.

In the future, you may have more variables to check before allowing the user to fire the gun (e.g., if the screen was paused, or at the end of a level). It would be a good idea at this point to create a function that checks for all parameter values and then outputs a resulting decision. This output would then be checked globally by other functions (such as if it is possible to pause) and the `fireGun()` function when deciding whether to proceed.

Before we can test, we need to add the function into the `default.html` file. Reopen the `default.html` file. Type the following new line (in bold) and an addition to an existing line (modified text is in red):

```
<html>
 <head>
  <script src="js/jquery.js"></script>
  <script src="js/jquery-ui.js"></script>
  <script src="js/SZ_main.js"></script>
  <script src="js/SZ_setupContent.js"></script>
  <script src="js/SZ_movement.js"></script>
  <script src="js/ss.js"></script>
  <script src="js/SZ_SS.js"></script>
  <script src="js/SZ_touch.js"></script>
  <link href="css/SZ_master.css" rel="stylesheet" />
 </head>
 <body>
  <div id="SZ_maincontent">
   <img id="SZO_0" src="images/SZ_background_image.jpg"
   onmousemove="rotateGun(event)"onmousedown="fireGun(event)" />
   <div id="SZO_1" ></div>
   <div id="SZO_2" >
    <img  src="images/SZ_reload.png"
    onmousedown="reloadGun(event)" />
   </div>
   <div id="SZO_3" >
```

```
    <img src="images/SZ_score.png" />
  </div>
 </div>
</body>
</html>
```

Save the file and then close it. Go back to the `My_Work_Files` folder and double-click the `default.html` file. Now click anywhere on the screen. The gun should animate the firing sequence.

By now, the gun should be doing the following:

- Moving in response to the mouse on the screen

- Reloading when the user clicks the Reload button

- Firing when the user clicks anywhere on our play area of the screen

In this section, we invoked a specific set of sprite animation using the following line:

$("#SZ0_1").animateSprite("play", "fire");

How does the system know what to do with `"fire"`? If you go back to the code, notice we wrote the following:

animations: {
          static: [0],
          reload: [1,2,3,4,5,6,7,8,9,10,11,12,13,14,15,16,17,
             18,19,20,21,22,23],

```
    fire: [24,25,26,27,28],
  },
```

One of the animations we defined was called "fire" and it was images 24 to 28 of the individual sprite images.

Note that we inserted two mouse events into an image tag with the following code:

```
<img id="SZ0_0" src="images/SZ_background_image.jpg"
onmousemove="rotateGun(event)"  onmousedown="fireGun(event)" />
```

This is entirely possible because (a) you can have multiple mouse events defined for an element, and (b) the two mouse events do not conflict with each other.

One Last Thing...

You may have noticed that when you click the Reload button, the cursor remains as a crosshair. It would be nice if it changes back to a more appropriate cursor, which is more intuitive and makes for a better gameplay experience.

We can do this by changing the CSS. You will now need to reopen the SZ_master.css file and type the following new line (in bold):

```
html {

    height: 100%;

  }
body {

    padding: 0 0 0 0;

    margin: 0;
    user-select: none;
```

```
        cursor: crosshair;
    }
img  {
        max-width: 100%;
        height: auto;
        user-drag: none;
        user-select: none;
        -moz-user-select: none;
        -webkit-user-drag: none;
        -webkit-user-select: none;
        -ms-user-select: none;
    }
#SZO_0 {
        position: fixed;
        top: 0;
        left: 0;
        min-width: 100%;
        min-height: 100%;
    }
 #SZO_1 {
        position: fixed;
        bottom: 0;
        right: 0;
}
 #SZO_2 {
        position: fixed;
        top: 0;
        left: 0;
        cursor: pointer;
}
```

```
#SZO_3 {
        position: fixed;
        top: 0;
        right: 0;
}
```

Save the file and then close it. Go back to the My_Work_Files folder and double-click the default.html file.

Now when you move the cursor over the Reload button, it should change instantly into a normal "hand" image. Similarly, when you move the mouse away from the Reload button, it should change back to the cursor image.

The next chapter introduces the zombies to our game, which finally gives our players some interactivity.

The cursor does not change to a pointer when it's over the Reload button?

This error may be from the HTML file. First, check that you have inserted the this line

```
cursor: pointer;
```

in the #SZO_2 section.

If you have done this already, then we need to take a look at the default.html file. Ensure that you have replaced all the image tags into the div tags as indicated.

For example, what used to be

```
<img id="SZo_1" src="images/SZ_gun.png" />
<img id="SZo_2" src="images/SZ_reload.png" />
<img id="SZo_3" src="images/SZ_score.png" />
```

Should now be

```
<div id="SZo_1" ></div>
 <div id="SZo_2" >
  <img  src="images/SZ_reload.png"
  onmousedown="reloadGun(event)" />
 </div>
 <div id="SZo_3" >
  <img src="images/SZ_score.png" />
 </div>
```

If your code is still not working, then please do not hesitate to message me on Twitter @zarrarchishti.

CHAPTER 6

Where Are the Zombies?

"Measuring programming progress by lines of code is like measuring aircraft building progress by weight."

Bill Gates

Let's recap what our zombies need to do in our game. We need six zombies that will walk toward the screen. Each zombie has a sprite sheet with its walking animation. When a zombie reaches the end of its animation toward the screen, it needs to reset to its original position.

Creating a Zombie: Part 1

First, we need to add the following four sprite sheets to your image folder:

- zombiesSS_1.png: the scientist zombie walking
- zombiesSS_2.png: the female zombie walking
- zombiesSS_3.png: the male zombie walking
- SZ_bubble.png: the three zombies stuck in a bubble

85

© Zarrar Chishti 2017
Z. Chishti, *Cross Over to HTML5 Game Development*,
https://doi.org/10.1007/978-1-4842-3291-0_6

Go to the `images` folder in the `Raw Images` folder of the `My_Work_Files` folder. Locate the files named `zombiesSS_1.png`, `zombiesSS_2.png`, `zombiesSS_3.png`, and `SZ_bubble.png`, and copy these to the `Images` folder, which should now look like this:

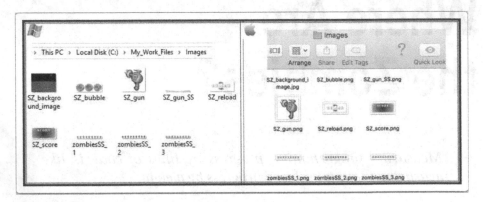

Creating a Zombie: Part 2

By the end of this section, you will see a zombie at the edge of our planet. To do this, we need to code a zombie from scratch. Again, I apologize in advance, as there will be a fair bit of coding. However, the excitement of seeing your very own zombie appearing on the screen is worth all the hard work.

Open the `SZ_zombie_movement.js` file, which should be completely blank. Type the following lines:

```
//let's create a zombie
function SZ_createZombie(whichOne){

 //create a new div to hold the zombie SS
    var div = document.createElement('div');

 //we need to hard code the CSS styles we want
    div.setAttribute('style','position: fixed; top:0; left:0;')
```

```
//we want to position our zombie exactly at the tip of the planet
  var top_position= $('#SZ0_0').height() * 0.435;
```

```
//Xpos can be anywhere on our x axis
  var left_position = Math.floor(Math.random() *
  ($('#SZ0_0').width())-(ratio*50)) + (ratio*50);
```

```
//let's position our zombie
  div.style.left = left_position+'px'; div.style.top =
  top_position+'px';
```

```
//give it an id
  div.id = 'zombie'+whichOne;
```

```
//finally let's add our zombie to the screen
  document.body.appendChild(div);
```

```
//put this new zombie through our SS function
  setup_zombie_SS(whichOne);

}
```

You can now save and close this file.

We have introduced a few new elements in the code, which are explored in the "Further Information" section.

Before we do further coding, we need to link this new file to our default.html file. Reopen the default.html file and type the following new line, along with the extra bit of text in one of our existing lines (all the new text is in bold):

```
<html>
 <head>
  <script src="js/jquery.js"></script>
  <script src="js/jquery-ui.js"></script>
  <script src="js/SZ_main.js"></script>
  <script src="js/SZ_setupContent.js"></script>
  <script src="js/SZ_movement.js"></script>
  <script src="js/ss.js"></script>
  <script src="js/SZ_SS.js"></script>
  <script src="js/SZ_touch.js"></script>
  <script src="js/SZ_zombie_movement.js"></script>
  <link href="css/SZ_master.css" rel="stylesheet" />
 </head>
 <body>
  <div id="SZ_maincontent">
   <img id="SZO_0" src="images/SZ_background_image.jpg"
   onmousemove="rotateGun(event)"  onmousedown="fireGun(event)" />
   <div id="SZO_1" ></div>
   <div id="SZO_2" >
    <img  src="images/SZ_reload.png"
    onmousedown="reloadGun(event)" />
   </div>
   <div id="SZO_3" >
    <img src="images/SZ_score.png" />
   </div>
  </div>
 </body>
</html>
```

Save the file and then close it. Now we can go ahead and further develop our zombie sprite sheets. Reopen the SZ_SS file in your js folder.

Type the following new lines (all new text is in bold):

```
//We need a one stop function that will allow us to process
sprite sheets
function setup_SpriteSheet(div_name, image_name, no_of_frames,
widthx, heightx) {

 //need the ratio of the container's width/height
   var imageOrgRatio =  $(div_name).height() / $(div_name).
   width() ;

 //need to ensure no trailing decimals
   var ratio2 = Math.round(ratio * 10) / 10;

 //check that the width is completely divisible by the no of
 frames
   var newDivisible = Math.round((widthx * ratio2) / no_of_
   frames);

 //the new width will be the number of frames multiplied by our
 new divisible
   var newWidthx = newDivisible * no_of_frames;

 //also the new height will be our ratio times the height of
 the div containing our image
   var newHeightx = heightx * ratio2;

 //apply our new width to our CSS
   $(div_name).css('width', (newWidthx));

 //apply our new height to our CSS
   $(div_name).css('height', newHeightx);
 //
```

```
//take the image name and apply as a background image to our div
    $(div_name).css('background-image', 'url(' + image_name + ')');

//finally we need to apply a background size remembering we
need to multiply width by the no of frames
    $(div_name).css('background-size', newWidthx * no_of_frames
    + 'px ' + newHeightx + 'px');
}

//setup the Gun
function setup_gun_SS(){
 //first let's setup our gun SS
    setup_SpriteSheet("#SZ0_1","Images/SZ_gun_SS.png",28,150,150);
 //need to access a special function in our js/ss.js file
    $("#SZ0_1").animateSprite({
        fps: 10,
        animations: {
            static: [0],
            reload: [1,2,3,4,5,6,7,8,9,10,11,12,13,14,15,16,17,
                     18,19,20,21,22,23],
            fire: [24,25,26,27,28],
        },
        duration: 50,
        loop: false,
        complete: function () {
            // use complete only when you set animations with
            'loop: false'
            //alert("animation End");
            //we need to reset our universal flag
              canIclick=0;
        }
    });
}
```

```
//setup a newly created zombie
function setup_zombie_SS(whichOne){

  //let's identify what type of zombie we should create
    var type_zombie = [1,2,3,1,2,3];

  //let's setup a speed for each type of zombie
    var speed_zombie = [100,50,150];

  //first let's setup our zombie SS

    setup_SpriteSheet("#zombie"+whichOne,"Images/
    zombiesSS_"+type_zombie[whichOne-1]+".png",9,20,20);
  //need to access a special function in our js/ss.js file
    $("#zombie"+whichOne).animateSprite({
        fps: 10,
        animations: {
            static: [0,1,2,3,4,5,6,7],
        },
        duration: speed_zombie[type_zombie[whichOne-1]-1],
        loop: true,
        complete: function () {
            // use complete only when you set animations with
            'loop: false'
            //alert("animation End");
        }
    });
}
```

Save the file and then close it.

You will have noticed that we keep repeating the code to set up a sprite sheet in various JavaScript files. I have done it like this to keep the code flowing linearly; however, you may decide to create one file for all sprite sheet operations.

We now need to call this function in our setup file to create a zombie. Reopen the SZ_setupContent file in your js folder and type the following new lines (all new text is in bold):

```
//main function
  function main_call_setupContent() {
  //need to resize all elements
  //first we set their normal sizes in CSS

  //Gun
   $('#SZO_1').css('width', 150 * ratio);
   $('#SZO_1').css('height', 150 * ratio);

  //Reload Button
   $('#SZO_2').css('width', 200 * ratio);
   $('#SZO_2').css('height', 90 * ratio);

  //Score
   $('#SZO_3').css('width', 235 * ratio);
   $('#SZO_3').css('height', 100 * ratio);

  //Any sprite sheets?
   //Our Gun
      setup_gun_SS();

  //Create a zombie
    SZ_createZombie(1);

}
```

We are now ready to test! Save all the files and then close them. Go back to your My_Work_Files folder and double-click the default.html file. What you should see is a scientist zombie at the edge of the planet surface.

If you click your browser's Refresh button (alternatively, you could press F5), the zombie should appear in a different location (yet still at the edge of the planet surface). Continue to refresh a few times and test this behavior.

We have now managed to spawn a zombie in our game! Our next step will be to make our zombie come toward us.

Did it not work? Here are a few areas to check:

- Check that you have linked the `SZ_zombie_movement. js` file correctly in your `default.html`.

- We are using arrays for the first time (see the "Further Information" section about what arrays are). Ensure that you are using the square brackets located next to the P key on your keyboard.

- Finally, ensure that the following line is as coded exactly as shown: `setup_SpriteSheet("#zombie"+whichOne, "Images/zombiesSS_"+type_zombie[whichOne-1]+". png",9,20,20);`

If your code is still not working, then please do not hesitate to message me on Twitter @zarrarchishti.

Three exciting features in this section. Let's explore them a little more.

- **Creating a `div` dynamically**. What does *dynamically* mean? It means that the `div` for the zombie was generated when the game was running; that is, we did not code a `div` for the zombie in the `default.html` file where we have all of our other `div`s. The main reason for doing it this way is to generate multiple zombies by calling one function rather than writing out each `div` manually.

- **Arrays**. If you were reading a conventional coding book in any computer language, you would have been introduced to arrays on day 1. However, I think it is better to learn it now because you just had a practical use for one, and therefore you are able to understand the explanation better. Let's take a quick look at one of our arrays.

```
var type_zombie = [1,2,3,1,2,3];
```

- `var` declares the array as a new element.

- `type_zombie` is the name of the array.

- [ ] anything in these brackets are the contents of the array, separated by commas

  We have an array of six integers starting with the number 1 and ending with the number 3.

We used a couple of math functions in our coding. Let's have a look at some of them.

- `Math.random()` is a special JavaScript function to generate a random number. This random number was used (with some manipulation) to randomly place our zombie.

- `Math.floor()` is a function that essentially rounds down a number; for example, 45.89 would return 45. Incidentally, the opposite of this function (i.e., rounding up) is `Math.ceil()`, so 45.89 would return 46.

Moving the Zombie Closer

To bring our zombie toward us, we will use JavaScript. The code will do two animations simultaneously. First, it will pull the zombie down the screen. Second, the zombie will be scaled to look larger. By doing these two animations together, we give the illusion of the zombie walking toward us.

Open the SZ_zombie_movement.js file and type the following new lines (all new text is in bold):

```
//let's create a zombie
function SZ_createZombie(whichOne){

 //create a new div to hold the zombie SS
   var div = document.createElement('div');

 //we need to hard code the CSS styles we want
   div.setAttribute('style','position: fixed; top:0; left:0;')

 //we want to position our zombie exactly at the tip of the planet
   var top_position= $('#SZO_0').height() * 0.435;

 //Xpos can be anywhere on our x axis
   var left_position = Math.floor(Math.random() * ($('#SZO_0').
   width())-(ratio*50)) + (ratio*50);

 //let's position our zombie
   div.style.left = left_position+'px'; div.style.top =
   top_position+'px';

 //give it an id
   div.id = 'zombie'+whichOne;

 //finally let's add our zombie to the screen
   document.body.appendChild(div);

 //put this new zombie through our SS function
  setup_zombie_SS(whichOne);
```

```
//put this new zombie through our animate function
  SZ_animateZombie(whichOne);

}

//let's animate our zombie towards us
function SZ_animateZombie(whichOne){

    //assign the speed for each of our zombies
    var timex =  [13000,8000,16000,14000,10000,18000];

    //assign a user friendly name for our div
    var $zombiex = $("#zombie"+whichOne);

    //work out the amount the zombie has to come towards us
    var amty =  ($(window).height()*0.7);// -($zombiex.
    height()*2));//topx);

    //each type of zombie will have their own walking style
    var ZS_ease = ['easeInSine','easeOutQuart','easeInOutQuad',
    'easeInSine','easeOutQuart','easeInOutQuad'];

    //finally we are ready to animate
      $zombiex.animate({
                //first bring our zombie slowly down the screen
                left:    amty+ "px",
        },{ easing:ZS_ease[whichOne-1],  duration:
        timex[whichOne-1],

          step: function(now, fx){
          //at each step we can manipulate the scale of
          our zombie
            if (fx.prop == "left") {
                //work out the amount to scale
                var xx = (fx.pos)*16;
                //apply the scale
                $(this).css('transform','scale('+xx+')');
```

```
        }
    }, complete: function () {
        }
    });
}
```

Save this file and then close it. Go back to the My_Work_Files folder and double-click the default.html file.

When the screen comes up, you should see the zombie coming toward you! Depending on your screen resolution, the zombie may overstep the edge or stop a little before it should. Do not worry about that; we will handle it in Chapter 8.

Next, let's look into creating all the zombies that we need for the game.

The following array has text values, but what are they?

```
var ZS_ease = ['easeInSine','easeOutQuart','easeInOutQuad','eas
eInSine','easeOutQuart','easeInOutQuad'];
```

These values are what we use for our *easing function*. An easing function specifies a zombie's rate of change over time. The simplest and most widely used easing value is a linear one. This is where the zombie moves at a constant speed for the duration of its walk. That would be a little boring and unrealistic, however.

We have a wide range of easing functions to choose from. The following are the ones that we will use:

- For our scientist zombie, `easeInSine`. It starts quite slowly and then accelerates for the rest of the journey. Here is a graph depicting the function:

- For our female zombie, `easeOutQuart`. There is no delay at the start; she begins abruptly and eases off near the end. Here is a graph depicting the function:

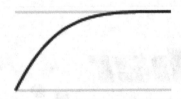

- For our male zombie, `easeInOutQuad`. There is a delay both at the start and at the finish. The midway section is fairly average as well. Here is a graph depicting the function:

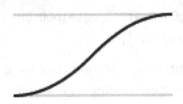

Creating All the Zombies

We will create six zombies for our game. We could create as many (or as few) as we want; however, we need to consider memory issues when creating a game. If we create too many zombies, the game may run out of computer memory. On the other hand, if we create too few, then the game may not be challenging enough. Essentially, it's all about finding the perfect parameters for the game and the player.

Open the SZ_setupContent.js file in the js folder. First, locate the following two lines and remove them:

```
//Create a zombie
    SZ_createZombie(1);
```

Type the following new lines (all new text is in bold):

```
//main function
  function main_call_setupContent() {
  //need to resize all elements
  //first we set their normal sizes in CSS

  //Gun
  $('#SZO_1').css('width', 150 * ratio);
  $('#SZO_1').css('height', 150 * ratio);

  //Reload Button
  $('#SZO_2').css('width', 200 * ratio);
  $('#SZO_2').css('height', 90 * ratio);

  //Score
  $('#SZO_3').css('width', 235 * ratio);
  $('#SZO_3').css('height', 100 * ratio);

  //Any sprite sheets?
    //Our Gun
      setup_gun_SS();
```

```
//Create all our 6 zombies
 for (i = 1; i < 7; i++) {
 //this will get called 6 times
 SZ_createZombie(i);
 }
}
```

Save this file and then close it.

For the purposes of this book, we have determined to keep the maximum number of zombies to six. To keep this function future-proof, however, I recommend revisiting it to accept the maximum number of zombies as a parameter. You would replace the 7 in the for loop with this parameter name.

Go back to the My_Work_Files folder and double-click the default. html file.

When the screen comes up, you should see all six zombies make their way toward the screen. You will see not only the scientist zombie but also the female and the male zombies too. I should note that their speed is relative to what we discussed in Chapter 1.

I am noting the following concerns:

- The zombies overlap each other.

- The gun is hidden behind the zombies.

- The mouse cursor does not turn into crosshairs when over a zombie.

I illustrated the first two points in the following screenshot:

Do not worry about these issues too much at this stage. All of these concerns are addressed in Chapter 8. Next, we will look at recycling the life of our zombie so that once it finishes, the element is ready for our program to use again.

Further Information

In this section, we came across a for loop to create our six zombies:

```
for (i = 1; i < 7; i++) {
```

By using this loop, we eliminated the need to write the same code to create a zombie six times. If that had been the case, then imagine if we were to create 100 zombies!

As shown in the example, loops are essential if you want to run the same code over and over again with a different value.

Here are four different kinds of loops that we can use in our game:

- `for` loops through a block of code a number of times

- `for/in` loops through the properties of an object

- `while` loops through a block of code while a specified condition is true

- `do/while` also loops through a block of code while a specified condition is true

Generating a Zombie Life Cycle

As you can see, the zombies remain on the screen once they reach the screen. Eventually, we will want to end the game if any zombie reaches the screen. For now, we are happy to just send them back to the start.

Open the `SZ_zombie_movement.js` file and type the following new lines (all new text is in bold):

```
//let's create a zombie
function SZ_createZombie(whichOne){

 //create a new div to hold the zombie SS
   var div = document.createElement('div');

 //we need to hard code the CSS styles we want
   div.setAttribute('style','position: fixed; top:0; left:0;')

 //we want to position our zombie exactly at the tip of the
 planet
   var top_position= $('#SZ0_0').height() * 0.435;

 //Xpos can be anywhere on our x axis
   var left_position = Math.floor(Math.random() * ($('#SZ0_0').
   width())-(ratio*50)) + (ratio*50);
```

```
//let's position our zombie
  div.style.left = left_position+'px'; div.style.top =
  top_position+'px';

//give it an id
  div.id = 'zombie'+whichOne;

//finally let's add our zombie to the screen
  document.body.appendChild(div);

//put this new zombie through our SS function
  setup_zombie_SS(whichOne);

//put this new zombie through our animate function
  SZ_animateZombie(whichOne);

}


//let's animate our zombie towards us
function SZ_animateZombie(whichOne){

      //assign the speed for each of our zombies
      var timex =  [13000,8000,16000,14000,10000,18000];

      //assign a user friendly name for our div
      var $zombiex = $("#zombie"+whichOne);

      //reset the zombies scale value
      $zombiex.css('transform','scale('+0+')');

      //work out the amount the zombie has to come towards us
      var amty =  ($(window).height()*0.7);// -($zombiex.
      height()*2));//topx);

      //each type of zombie will have their own walking style
      var ZS_ease = ['easeInSine','easeOutQuart','easeInOutQuad',
        'easeInSine','easeOutQuart','easeInOutQuad'];
```

```
    //finally we are ready to animate
    $zombiex.delay(timex[whichOne-1]/3).animate({
            //first bring our zombie slowly down the screen
            left:    "+="+1+ "px",
    },{ easing:ZS_ease[whichOne-1],  duration:
    timex[whichOne-1],

        step: function(now, fx){
          //at each step we can manipulate the scale of
          our zombie
          if (fx.prop == "left") {
              //work out the amount to scale
              var xx = (fx.pos)*16;
          //do a check to see if we should end this animation
              if(xx>15){
                  //stop all animation
                  $(this).stop();
                  //call a function to reset this zombie
                  SZ_resetZombie(whichOne);
              } else {
                  //apply the scale
                  $(this).css('transform','scale('+xx+')');
              }
          }
        }, complete: function () {
          }
      });
}
//a function to completely reset our zombie
function SZ_resetZombie(whichOne){

    //assign a user friendly name for our div
    var $zombiex = $("#zombie"+whichOne);
```

```
//we want to position our zombie exactly at the tip of the
planet
  var top_position= $('#SZ0_0').height() * 0.435;

//Xpos can be anywhere on our x axis
  var left_position = Math.floor(Math.random() *
  ($('#SZ0_0').width())-(ratio*50)) + (ratio*50);

//let's re-position our zombie
  $zombiex.css({top: top_position+'px', left: left_
  position+'px'});

//finally let's make the zombie come towards the screen again
  SZ_animateZombie(whichOne);
}
```

Save this file and then close it.

Again, the function to reset the zombie needs to be future-proofed. I suggest placing all the possible parameters for a zombie's starting position in a separate file. In this function, we instruct the code to access the new file for instructions with possible parameters for different variances (e.g., if the user is in a higher level, the values could be different).

Go back to the My_Work_Files folder and double-click the default. html file.

When the screen comes up, you should see the zombies come to the screen as before but then disappear. When they reappear, they should appear in a different position when coming toward the screen.

In the next chapter, we look at taking a shot at our zombies.

Did it not work? This could be due to a few lines that we added around some existing code. Let's have a look.

The original line of code was

```
$zombiex. animate({
```

Make sure that the new line of code looks like this:

```
$zombiex.delay(timex[whichOne-1]/2).animate({
```

The original line of code was

```
//apply the scale
                    $(this).css('transform',
                    'scale('+xx+')');
```

Make sure that the new line of code looks like this:

```
//do a check to see if we should end this animation
                if(xx>15){
                    //stop all animation
                    $(this).stop();
                    //call a function to reset this zombie
                    SZ_resetZombie(whichOne);
                } else {
                    //apply the scale
                    $(this).css('transform',
                    'scale('+xx+')');
                }
            }
```

If your code is still not working, then please do not hesitate to message me on Twitter @zarrarchishti.

CHAPTER 7

Take a Shot: Part 2

"If you do it right, it will last forever"

Massimo Vignelli

The good news is that we are near the end. The slightly bad news is that there will be a fair bit of coding in this chapter. So what will we see at the end of this chapter?

- The gun will be able to fire on zombies.

- The zombies will register the hits. If the maximum number of hits is reached, a zombie will turn into a bubble.

- The bubble zombie will fly away into the distance.

- We need to keep track of the number of times the gun has been fired, and require the user to reload when the maximum has been reached.

- Finally, if a zombie reaches the screen, we need to declare the game over.

Hitting a Zombie

You may have noticed that when you try to click a zombie, the gun does not fire. This is because we have not bound a mouse-click event to the zombie elements. We can place this mouse-click code in the function where we create each zombie.

© Zarrar Chishti 2017
Z. Chishti, *Cross Over to HTML5 Game Development*,
https://doi.org/10.1007/978-1-4842-3291-0_7

Open the SZ_zombie_movement.js file and type the following new lines (all new text is in bold):

```
//let's create a zombie
function SZ_createZombie(whichOne){

 //create a new div to hold the zombie SS
   var div = document.createElement('div');

 //we need to hard code the CSS styles we want
   div.setAttribute('style','position: fixed; top:0; left:0;')

 //we want to position our zombie exactly at the tip of the planet
   var top_position= $('#SZ0_0').height() * 0.435;

 //Xpos can be anywhere on our x axis
   var left_position = Math.floor(Math.random() * ($('#SZ0_0').
   width())-(ratio*50)) + (ratio*50);

 //let's position our zombie
   div.style.left = left_position+'px'; div.style.top = top_
   position+'px';

 //give it an id
   div.id = 'zombie'+whichOne;

 //finally let's add our zombie to the screen
   document.body.appendChild(div);

 //put this new zombie through our SS function
  setup_zombie_SS(whichOne);

 //put this new zombie through our animate function
   SZ_animateZombie(whichOne);

 //bind the users mouse click to this zombie
 $("#zombie"+whichOne).bind('mousedown touchstart', function (e) {
```

```
        //first we want to fire the gun
        fireGun(event);
    });
}


//let's animate our zombie towards us
function SZ_animateZombie(whichOne){

    //assign the speed for each of our zombies
    var timex = [13000,8000,16000,14000,10000,18000];

    //assign a user friendly name for our div
    var $zombiex = $("#zombie"+whichOne);

    //reset the zombies scale value
     $zombiex.css('transform','scale('+0+')');

    //work out the amount the zombie has to come towards us
     var amty = ($(window).height()*0.7);// -($zombiex.
     height()*2));//topx);

    //each type of zombie will have their own walking style
     var ZS_ease = ['easeInSine','easeOutQuart','easeInOutQuad',
     'easeInSine','easeOutQuart','easeInOutQuad'];

    //finally we are ready to animate
      $zombiex.delay(timex[whichOne-1]/3).animate({
              //first bring our zombie slowly down the screen
              left:   "+="+1+ "px",
        },{ easing:ZS_ease[whichOne-1], duration:
        timex[whichOne-1],

            step: function(now, fx){
            //at each step we can manipulate the scale of
            our zombie
```

```
                    if (fx.prop == "left") {
                        //work out the amount to scale
                        var xx = (fx.pos)*16;
                    //do a check to see if we should end this
                    animation
                        if(xx>15){
                            //stop all animation
                            $(this).stop();
                            //call a function to reset this zombie
                            SZ_resetZombie(whichOne);
                        } else {
                            //apply the scale
                            $(this).css('transform',
                            'scale('+xx+')');
                        }
                    }
                }, complete: function () {
                    }
            });
}
//a function to completely reset our zombie
function SZ_resetZombie(whichOne){

    //assign a user friendly name for our div
     var $zombiex = $("#zombie"+whichOne);

    //we want to position our zombie exactly at the tip of the
    planet
     var top_position= $('#SZ0_0').height() * 0.435;

    //Xpos can be anywhere on our x axis
     var left_position = Math.floor(Math.random() *
     ($('#SZ0_0').width())-(ratio*50)) + (ratio*50);
```

```
//let's re-position our zombie
$zombiex.css({top: top_position+'px', left: left_
position+'px'});

//finally let's make the zombie come towards the screen
again
SZ_animateZombie(whichOne);
}
```

Navigate to the menu, click File, and then click Save. You can now close this file.

We are now ready to test! Go back to the My_Work_Files folder and double-click the default.html file. You should see the gun firing when you click over any of the zombies coming toward the screen.

This was made possible by adding 'mousedown touchstart' events to each zombie's div. When revisiting this project, you may wish to consider installing a "headshot" type of feature. For this to work, you need to do the following:

1. Place a div within the zombie's div that defines its head.

2. Place the same 'mousedown touchstart' events to this new div, which should override the outer div's functionality.

3. If this new div is hit, then give the user more points.

4. You may want to consider awarding the maximum hits if the div is hit; for example, if it usually takes three hits to kill a zombie (this functionality is added in the next section), only one of the headshots is sufficient.

111

In earlier chapters, we bound mouse events by adding them to the image tag; for example

```
<img id="SZO_O" onmousemove="rotateGun(event)"
src="images/SZ_background_image.jpg" />
```

In this section, however, we needed to add a mouse event to our zombies, which are not created in our HTML page.

So just as we created the zombies dynamically, we have to bind the events to them at runtime as well. This was done by using JavaScript code, as follows:

```
$("#zombie"+whichOne).bind('mousedown touchstart', function (e) {
```

In this line, we have not only bound the mousedown event to each zombie, but also defined the instructions that execute when that event occurs.

Did the code not work? Check to see if you have typed whichOne (make sure that the O is a capital letter) in the new code that you have written.

When writing any code from this book, it is extremely important to be aware that JavaScript makes a sharp distinction between capital and lowercase letters.

JavaScript does not consider a variable named whichone to be the same as a variable named whichOne.

If the code is still not working, then please do not hesitate to message me on Twitter @zarrarchishti.

Making the Hits Count

Let's recap the number of hits each zombie will be able to take before "dying."

- Professor Z: two hits

- Belladonna: one hit

- Brad: three hits

To keep track of the number of hits each zombie has taken, we need to use an array. Also, we need to remember to reset each zombie's hit count when it resets.

Open the SZ_zombie_movement.js file and type the following new lines (all new text is in bold):

```
//let's create a zombie
function SZ_createZombie(whichOne){

//create a new div to hold the zombie SS
  var div = document.createElement('div');

//we need to hard code the CSS styles we want
  div.setAttribute('style','position: fixed; top:0; left:0;')

//we want to position our zombie exactly at the tip of the
planet
  var top_position= $('#SZ0_0').height() * 0.435;

//Xpos can be anywhere on our x axis
```

```
  var left_position = Math.floor(Math.random() * ($('#SZ0_0').
  width())-(ratio*50)) + (ratio*50);

//let's position our zombie
  div.style.left = left_position+'px'; div.style.top = top_
  position+'px';

//give it an id
  div.id = 'zombie'+whichOne;

//finally let's add our zombie to the screen
  document.body.appendChild(div);

//put this new zombie through our SS function
 setup_zombie_SS(whichOne);

//put this new zombie through our animate function
  SZ_animateZombie(whichOne);

//bind the users mouse click to this zombie
$("#zombie"+whichOne).bind('mousedown touchstart', function (e) {
        //first we want to fire the gun
         fireGun(event);
         //acknowledge the hit
          zombieHit(whichOne-1);
    });

}


//let's animate our zombie towards us
function SZ_animateZombie(whichOne){

    //assign the speed for each of our zombies
    var timex =  [13000,8000,16000,14000,10000,18000];

    //assign a user friendly name for our div
    var $zombiex = $("#zombie"+whichOne);
```

```
//reset the zombies scale value
$zombiex.css('transform','scale('+0+')');
```

```
//work out the amount the zombie has to come towards us
var amty =  ($(window).height()*0.7);// -($zombiex.
height()*2));//topx);
```

```
//each type of zombie will have their own walking style
var ZS_ease = ['easeInSine','easeOutQuart','easeInOutQuad',
'easeInSine','easeOutQuart','easeInOutQuad'];
```

```
//finally we are ready to animate
  $zombiex.delay(timex[whichOne-1]/3).animate({
            //first bring our zombie slowly down the screen
            left:    "+="+1+ "px",
    },{ easing:ZS_ease[whichOne-1],  duration:
    timex[whichOne-1],

        step: function(now, fx){
        //at each step we can manipulate the scale of
        our zombie
          if (fx.prop == "left") {
              //work out the amount to scale
              var xx = (fx.pos)*16;
          //do a check to see if we should end this
          animation
                if(xx>15){
                  //stop all animation
                 // $(this).stop();
                  //call a function to reset this zombie
                  SZ_resetZombie(whichOne);
                } else {
                  //apply the scale
                   $(this).css('transform',
                   'scale('+xx+')');
```

```
                        }
                    }
                }, complete: function () {
                    }
            });
}
//a function to completely reset our zombie
function SZ_resetZombie(whichOne){

    //reset this zombies hit counter
    zombieHits_counter[whichOne-1]=0;

    //assign a user friendly name for our div
    var $zombiex = $("#zombie"+whichOne);

    //we need to stop this zombies animations
    $zombiex.stop();

    //we want to position our zombie exactly at the tip of the
    planet
    var top_position= $('#SZ0_0').height() * 0.435;

    //Xpos can be anywhere on our x axis
    var left_position = Math.floor(Math.random() *
    ($('#SZ0_0').width())-(ratio*50)) + (ratio*50);

    //let's re-position our zombie
    $zombiex.css({top: top_position+'px',
    left: left_position+'px'});

    //finally let's make the zombie come towards the screen
    again
    SZ_animateZombie(whichOne);
}
```

Save and close this file.

If you are developing levels for this game in the future, you want to add a check before resetting the zombie. For example, if the result of killing a zombie is a new level, then rather than just resetting that particular zombie, you want to reset all the zombies. I would even go as far as making this operation its own function, which performed all of these checks.

Open the SZ_touch.js file in the js folder. Type the following new lines (all new text is in bold):

```javascript
//We need a flag to keep track to avoid repetition of
animations before the first has finished
var canIclick= 0;

//this function is called to reload our gun
function reloadGun(e) {
 //Let's check if we can allow this to occur
   if(canIclick== 0){
     //looks like we can so we better set our flag
       canIclick=1;
       $("#SZO_1").animateSprite("play", "reload");
    }
}

//this function is called to fire our gun
function fireGun(e) {
 //Let's check if we can allow this to occur
   if(canIclick== 0){
     //looks like we can so we better set our flag
       canIclick=1;
       $("#SZO_1").animateSprite("play", "fire");
    }
}

//array to keep track of the zombie hits
 var zombieHits_counter = [0,0,0,0,0,0];
```

```
//array for each zombies limit
 var zombieHits_limits = [2,1,3,2,1,3];

//this function will keep track of the zombie hits and act
accordingly
function zombieHit(whichOne){

 //increment the counter
  zombieHits_counter[whichOne]++;

 //check to see if this zombie has reached its limit
  if(zombieHits_counter[whichOne] >= zombieHits_
  limits[whichOne]){
    //reset this zombie
     SZ_resetZombie(whichOne+1);
   }
}
```

Save and close this file. We are now ready to test! Go back to the My_Work_Files folder and double-click the default.html file.

Now, the zombies should reset before they reach the screen when we have fired on them the correct number of times. So if we fire once on the female zombie, she should reset immediately. Similarly, if we fire three times on the male zombie, he should reset. Finally, if we fire twice on the scientist zombie, then he should reset.

Next, I introduce our bubble zombies.

We used a couple of techniques to keep track and compare values in our code. Let's take a closer look at some of them.

```
var ZS_ease = zombieHits_counter[whichOne]++;
```

The ++ is an assignment operator that adds one to the current value of the variable.

Next, let's look at how we checked to see if the maximum number of hits had been reached.

```
if(zombieHits_counter[whichOne] >= zombieHits_limits[whichOne]){
```

An if statement is what we call a *conditional statement*. Conditional statements are used when you want to perform different actions on different decisions. So in this case, *if* the zombie has had the maximum number of hits, *then* we want to reset it; *otherwise*, do nothing.

And, you see >= in the statement, which means if the first value is *greater than or equal to* the second value. Here are some other conditional statements we could use for other instances:

- <= (less than or equal to)

- == (equal to)

- < (less than)

- > (greater than)

- != (not equal to)

Zombie Down!

When a zombie has been hit the maximum number of times, it is reset. We also need the zombie to appear in a bubble, however, to give the illusion that the zombie has been subdued and dealt with in the game.

To do this, the following needs to completed.

1. Create six bubble zombie elements that are ready to be deployed when needed.

2. Before resetting a zombie, activate its counter
    bubble zombie.

3. Make sure that the bubble zombie has the same
    scale and location values to make it seem as if the
    walking zombie has been transformed into the
    bubble.

4. Finally, we want the bubble zombie to float away
    into space.

Part 1: Create Six Bubble Zombie Elements

To create the six bubble zombies, we need to open the SZ_zombie_
movement.js file and type the following new lines (all new text is in bold):

```
//let's create a zombie
function SZ_createZombie(whichOne){

 //create a new div to hold the zombie SS
   var div = document.createElement('div');
 //and another for the bubble zombie SS
   var div2 = document.createElement('div');

 //we need to hard code the CSS styles we want
   div.setAttribute('style','position: fixed; top:0; left:0;')
 //and the same for our bubble zombie
   div2.setAttribute('style','position: fixed; top:0; left:0;')

 //we want to position our zombie exactly at the tip of the
 planet
   var top_position= $('#SZ0_0').height() * 0.435;

 //Xpos can be anywhere on our x axis
   var left_position = Math.floor(Math.random() * ($('#SZ0_0').
   width())-(ratio*50)) + (ratio*50);
```

```
//let's position our zombie
  div.style.left = left_position+'px'; div.style.top = top_
  position+'px';
//and the same for our bubble zombie
  div2.style.left = left_position+'px'; div2.style.top = top_
  position+'px';

//give it an id
  div.id = 'zombie'+whichOne;
//also for our bubble zombie
  div2.id = 'bubble_zombie'+whichOne;

//finally let's add our zombie to the screen
  document.body.appendChild(div);
//finally add in our bubble zombie to the screen too
  document.body.appendChild(div2);

//put this new zombie through our SS function
 setup_zombie_SS(whichOne);

//put this new zombie through our animate function
 SZ_animateZombie(whichOne);

//bind the users mouse click to this zombie
$("#zombie"+whichOne).bind('mousedown touchstart', function (e) {
    //first we want to fire the gun
      fireGun(event);
    //acknowledge the hit
      zombieHit(whichOne-1);
  });

}

//let's animate our zombie towards us
function SZ_animateZombie(whichOne){
```

```
//assign the speed for each of our zombies
var timex =  [13000,8000,16000,14000,10000,18000];

//assign a user friendly name for our div
var $zombiex = $("#zombie"+whichOne);

//reset the zombies scale value
 $zombiex.css('transform','scale('+0+')');

//work out the amount the zombie has to come towards us
 var amty =  ($(window).height()*0.7);// -($zombiex.
 height()*2));//topx);

//each type of zombie will have their own walking style
 var ZS_ease = ['easeInSine','easeOutQuart','easeInOutQuad',
 'easeInSine','easeOutQuart','easeInOutQuad'];

//finally we are ready to animate
    $zombiex.delay(timex[whichOne-1]/3).animate({
           //first bring our zombie slowly down the screen
           left:    "+="+1+ "px",
      },{ easing:ZS_ease[whichOne-1],  duration:
      timex[whichOne-1],

          step: function(now, fx){
             //at each step we can manipulate the scale of
             our zombie
             if (fx.prop == "left") {
                 //work out the amount to scale
                 var xx = (fx.pos)*16;
             //do a check to see if we should end this
             animation
                    if(xx>15){
                      //stop all animation
                      // $(this).stop();
```

```
                    //call a function to reset this zombie
                    SZ_resetZombie(whichOne);
                } else {
                    //apply the scale
                    $(this).css('transform',
                    'scale('+xx+')');
                }
            }
        }, complete: function () {
        }
    });
}
//a function to completely reset our zombie
function SZ_resetZombie(whichOne){

    //reset this zombies hit counter
    zombieHits_counter[whichOne-1]=0;

    //assign a user friendly name for our div
    var $zombiex = $("#zombie"+whichOne);

    //we need to stop this zombies animations
    $zombiex.stop();

    //we want to position our zombie exactly at the tip of the
    planet
    var top_position= $('#SZ0_0').height() * 0.435;

    //Xpos can be anywhere on our x axis
    var left_position = Math.floor(Math.random() *
    ($('#SZ0_0').width())-(ratio*50)) + (ratio*50);

    //let's re-position our zombie
    $zombiex.css({top: top_position+'px', left: left_
    position+'px'});
```

```
//finally let's make the zombie come towards the screen
again
 SZ_animateZombie(whichOne);
}
```

Save and close this file.

appendChild() is an interesting method used in this code. This method appends a node as the last child of another node. So in our case, we are adding our zombie's div to the end of our HTML body.

If in the future, you need to add an element, but not as the last child. You may wish to use insertBefore() rather than appendChild(). The insertBefore() method inserts a node as a child, right before an existing child, which you specify.

Before we can test to see our newly created bubble zombie divs, we need to add their sprite sheet functionality.

To do this, we now need to open the SZ_SS.js file in our js folder. Type the following new lines (all new text is in bold):

```
//We need a one stop function that will allow us to process
sprite sheets
function setup_SpriteSheet(div_name, image_name, no_of_frames,
widthx, heightx) {

 //need the ratio of the container's width/height
   var imageOrgRatio =  $(div_name).height() / $(div_name).
   width() ;

 //need to ensure no trailing decimals
   var ratio2 = Math.round(ratio * 10) / 10;

 //check that the width is completely divisible by the no of
 frames
   var newDivisible = Math.round((widthx * ratio2) / no_of_
   frames);
```

//the new width will be the number of frames multiplied by our
new divisible
```
  var newWidthx = newDivisible * no_of_frames;
```

//also the new height will be our ratio times the height of
the div containing our image
```
  var newHeightx = heightx * ratio2;
```

//apply our new width to our CSS
```
  $(div_name).css('width', (newWidthx));
```

//apply our new height to our CSS
```
  $(div_name).css('height', newHeightx);
//
```
//take the image name and apply as a background image to our div
```
  $(div_name).css('background-image', 'url(' + image_name + ')');
```

//finally we need to apply a background size remembering we
need to multiply width by the no of frames
```
  $(div_name).css('background-size', newWidthx * no_of_frames
  + 'px ' + newHeightx + 'px');
}
```

//setup the Gun
```
function setup_gun_SS(){
```
//first let's apply our gun to our SS function
```
  setup_SpriteSheet("#SZ0_1","Images/SZ_gun_SS.png",28,150,150);
```
//need to access a special function in our js/ss.js file
```
  $("#SZ0_1").animateSprite({
      fps: 10,
      animations: {
          static: [0],
          reload: [1,2,3,4,5,6,7,8,9,10,11,12,13,14,15,16,17,
                  18,19,20,21,22,23],
          fire: [24,25,26,27,28],
```

```
        },
        duration: 50,
        loop: false,
        complete: function () {
            // use complete only when you set animations with
            'loop: false'
            //alert("animation End");
            //we need to reset our universal flag
              canIclick=0;
        }
    });
}

//setup a newly created zombie
function setup_zombie_SS(whichOne){

 //let's identify what type of zombie we should create
   var type_zombie = [1,2,3,1,2,3];

 //let's setup a speed for each type of zombie
   var speed_zombie = [100,50,150];

 //first let's setup our zombie SS

setup_SpriteSheet("#zombie"+whichOne,"Images/zombiesSS_"+type_
zombie[whichOne-1]+".png",9,20,20);
 //need to access a special function in our js/ss.js file
    $("#zombie"+whichOne).animateSprite({
        fps: 10,
        animations: {
            static: [0,1,2,3,4,5,6,7],
        },
        duration: speed_zombie[type_zombie[whichOne-1]-1],
        loop: true,
```

```
        complete: function () {
            // use complete only when you set animations with
            'loop: false'
            //alert("animation End");
        }
    });
//now let's setup our bubble zombie SS
setup_SpriteSheet("#bubble_zombie"+whichOne,"Images/SZ_bubble.
png",3,20,20);
//need to access a special function in our js/ss.js file
    $("#bubble_zombie"+whichOne).animateSprite({
        fps: 10,
        animations: {
            z1: [type_zombie[whichOne-1]-1],
        },
        duration: 1,
        loop: false,
        complete: function () {
            // use complete only when you set animations with
            'loop: false'
            //alert("animation End");
        }
    });
}
```

Save and close this file.

Although we have touched on this before, using the alert() command is extremely useful when trying to pinpoint where a problem may lie in your code. In the preceding code, you see a commented alert() statement. At some point, I may have had some issues with this function's completion function triggering. By placing this alert() statement, I was able to test whether the function's completion timing was accurate.

As always, remember to remove (or comment out) all `alert()` statements.

Now we are ready to test! Go back to the `My_Work_Files` folder and double-click the `default.html` file.

Before the zombies come darting toward the screen, you should initially see six bubble zombies randomly placed along the planet's edge.

Did the code not work? Check to see if you have typed `div2` in the new code you have written in `SZ_zombie_movement.js`.

Also in the new code for `SZ_SS.js`, make sure that you have typed `bubble_zombie` and not just `zombie` (as per the preceding code).

If the code is still not working, then please do not hesitate to message me on Twitter `@zarrarchishti`.

Part 2: Activate the Counter Bubble Zombie

In this section, we concentrate on replacing the walking zombie with our new bubble zombie when the maximum number of hits has been reached. Also, we have to make sure that the corresponding bubble zombie is *not* shown until the maximum number of hits is reached.

First, open the SZ_touch.js file in the js folder. Modify the following line in bold:

```
//We need a flag to keep track to avoid repetition of
animations before the first has finished
var canIclick= 0;

//this function is called to reload our gun
function reloadGun(e) {
 //Let's check if we can allow this to occur
   if(canIclick== 0){
     //looks like we can so we better set our flag
       canIclick=1;
       $("#SZO_1").animateSprite("play", "reload");
   }
}

//this function is called to fire our gun
function fireGun(e) {
 //Let's check if we can allow this to occur
   if(canIclick== 0){
     //looks like we can so we better set our flag
       canIclick=1;
       $("#SZO_1").animateSprite("play", "fire");
   }
}
```

```
//array to keep track of the zombie hits
 var zombieHits_counter = [0,0,0,0,0,0];
//array for each zombies limit
 var zombieHits_limits = [2,1,3,2,1,3];

//this function will keep track of the zombie hits and act
accordingly
function zombieHit(whichOne){

 //increment the counter
  zombieHits_counter[whichOne]++;

 //check to see if this zombie has reached its limit
  if(zombieHits_counter[whichOne] >= zombieHits_limits[whichOne]){
    //reset this zombie
    SZ_resetZombie(whichOne+1,1);
   }
}
```

Save and close this file. Open the SZ_zombie_movement.js file. Carefully modify some old lines and type the following new lines (all modified and new text is in bold):

```
//let's create a zombie
function SZ_createZombie(whichOne){

 //create a new div to hold the zombie SS
   var div = document.createElement('div');
 //and another for the bubble zombie SS
   var div2 = document.createElement('div');

 //we need to hard code the CSS styles we want
   div.setAttribute('style','position: fixed; top:0; left:0;')
 //and the same for our bubble zombie
   div2.setAttribute('style','position: fixed; top:0; left:0;')
```

```
//we want to position our zombie exactly at the tip of the planet
   var top_position= $('#SZo_o').height() * 0.435;
```

```
//Xpos can be anywhere on our x axis
   var left_position = Math.floor(Math.random() * ($('#SZo_o').
   width())-(ratio*50)) + (ratio*50);
```

```
//record this left position
   leftx_zombie[whichOne-1]=left_position;
```

```
//let's position our zombie
   div.style.left = left_position+'px'; div.style.top = top_
   position+'px';
```
```
//and the same for our bubble zombie
   div2.style.left = left_position+'px'; div2.style.top = top_
   position+'px';
```

```
//give it an id
   div.id = 'zombie'+whichOne;
```
```
//also for our bubble zombie
   div2.id = 'bubble_zombie'+whichOne;
```

```
//finally let's add our zombie to the screen
   document.body.appendChild(div);
```
```
//finally add in our bubble zombie to the screen too
   document.body.appendChild(div2);
```

```
//put this new zombie through our SS function
 setup_zombie_SS(whichOne);
```

```
//put this new zombie through our animate function
 SZ_animateZombie(whichOne);
```

```
//hide the bubble zombies at the start
   $("#bubble_zombie"+whichOne).css('transform','scale('+0+')');
```

```
//bind the users mouse click to this zombie
$("#zombie"+whichOne).bind('mousedown touchstart', function (e) {
      //first we want to fire the gun
       fireGun(event);
      //acknowledge the hit
       zombieHit(whichOne-1);
   });
}

//we need to keep track of the current scale values
 var scalex_zombie =  [0,0,0,0,0,0];
//we also need to keep track of the left position
 var leftx_zombie =  [0,0,0,0,0,0];

//let's animate our zombie towards us
function SZ_animateZombie(whichOne){

    //assign the speed for each of our zombies
    var timex =  [13000,8000,16000,14000,10000,18000];

    //assign a user friendly name for our div
    var $zombiex = $("#zombie"+whichOne);

    //reset the zombies scale value
     $zombiex.css('transform','scale('+0+')');

    //work out the amount the zombie has to come towards us
     var amty =  ($(window).height()*0.7);// -($zombiex.
     height()*2));//topx);

    //each type of zombie will have their own walking style
     var ZS_ease = ['easeInSine','easeOutQuart','easeInOutQuad',
     'easeInSine','easeOutQuart','easeInOutQuad'];

    //finally we are ready to animate
     $zombiex.delay(timex[whichOne-1]/3).animate({
```

```
                //first bring our zombie slowly down the screen
            left:    "+="+0.001+ "px",
        },{ easing:ZS_ease[whichOne-1],
        duration: timex[whichOne-1],

            step: function(now, fx){
            //at each step we can manipulate the scale of
            our zombie
            if (fx.prop == "left") {
                //work out the amount to scale
                var xx = (fx.pos)*16;
                //do a check to see if we should end this
                animation
                    if(xx>15){
                        //stop all animation
                        // $(this).stop();
                        //call a function to reset this zombie
                        SZ_resetZombie(whichOne,0);
                    } else {
                        //apply the scale
                        $(this).css('transform',
                        'scale('+xx+')');
                        //record this new scale value
                        scalex_zombie[whichOne-1]=xx;
                    }
                }
            }, complete: function () {
                }
        });
}
//a function to completely reset our zombie
function SZ_resetZombie(whichOne, zombieBubble_generate){
```

```
//reset this zombies hit counter
 zombieHits_counter[whichOne-1]=0;
```

```
//assign a user friendly name for our div
 var $zombiex = $("#zombie"+whichOne);
```

```
//we need to stop this zombies animations
 $zombiex.stop();
```

```
//we want to position our zombie exactly at the tip of the
planet
 var top_position= $('#SZ0_0').height() * 0.435;
```

```
//should we generate a bubble zombie?
 if(zombieBubble_generate==1){
    //assign a user friendly name for our bubble zombie div
     var $bubble_zombiex = $("#bubble_zombie"+whichOne);
    //let's re-position our bubble zombie to our stored
    value
     $bubble_zombiex.css({top: top_position+'px',left:
     $zombiex.css("left")});
    //apply the scale
    $bubble_zombiex.css('transform',
     'scale('+scalex_zombie[whichOne-1]+')');
 }
```

```
//Xpos can be anywhere on our x axis
 var left_position = Math.floor(Math.random() *
($('#SZ0_0').width())-(ratio*50)) + (ratio*50);
```

```
//record this left position
 leftx_zombie[whichOne-1]=left_position;
```

```
//let's re-position our zombie
 $zombiex.css({top: top_position+'px', left:
 left_position+'px'});
```

```
//finally let's make the zombie come towards the screen again
SZ_animateZombie(whichOne);
}
```

You can now save and close this file. There is more code to write, however, let's quickly test what we have so far. Go back to the My_Work_ Files folder and double-click the default.html file. You should observe the following changes in our game:

- When the game starts, the bubble zombies in the distance have disappeared.

- When you reach the maximum number of hits on a zombie, it is replaced with a bubble zombie.

- The bubble zombie should correspond with the zombie you have just hit.

- The bubble zombie should be roughly the same size and position of the zombie it is replacing.

- Please note that you may notice that the zombies may stop coming all together. This has been done on purpose for some code that we will write later. For now, just refresh your browser (press F5) and the game should restart.

Next, we make the bubble zombies animate into space.

Did the code not work? First, check to see that you have modified the SZ_ resetZombie function to include an extra parameter (this code is in red):

```
function SZ_resetZombie(whichOne, zombieBubble_generate){
```

Also, the two times that we call this function need to be modified. Please make sure that your calls look like the following code:

In SZ_touch.js

```
SZ_resetZombie(whichOne+1,1);
```

And in SZ_zombie_movement.js

```
SZ_resetZombie(whichOne,0);
```

Finally, ensure that the following lines are placed exactly as shown (i.e., outside the function call):

```
//we need to keep track of the current scale values
var scalex_zombie =  [0,0,0,0,0,0];
//we also need to keep track of the left position
 var leftx_zombie =  [0,0,0,0,0,0];
//let's animate our zombie towards us
function SZ_animateZombie(whichOne){
```

If the code is still not working, then please do not hesitate to message me on Twitter @zarrarchishti.

___

Part 3: Animate the Bubble Zombies

In this final section, we animate each bubble zombie, which in turn triggers its corresponding zombie to start its animation toward the screen again. Then we provide a reset function for the bubble zombie so that it can be safely used again.

First, open the SZ_movement.js file and type the following new lines (all new text is in bold):

```
function rotateGun(e) {

//using the e value we can deduce the X co-ordinates
var xPos = e.clientX;

//We need to work out where the mouse cursor is as a percentage
of the width of the screen

//We will work this out by dividing the current X position
by the overall screen width which if you remember we put in
newWidth
var currentXPositionPercentage = xPos/newWidth;

//We now want to apply this to the maximum amount of rotation
which is 50 however the starting rotation is -15 not 0
var amountToRotate = -15 + (currentXPositionPercentage * 50);

//Let's rotate the gun!
  $("#SZO_1").css('transform', 'rotate('+amountToRotate+'deg)');

}

//movement for our bubble zombie
function bubbleZombie_flyAway(whichOne){

 //assign a user friendly name for our div
   var $zombiex = $("#bubble_zombie"+whichOne);

   //first it should animate upwards with a bounce
     $zombiex.animate({
               //bring our zombie up the screen
               top:    "-="+100*ratio+ "px",
         },{ easing:"easeOutElastic", duration: 400,

             complete: function () {
                 //now the final animation where the bubble
                 zombie disappears into space
```

137

```
        $(this).delay(150).animate({
        //slowly turn the alpha down
        opacity:   "-="+1,
        },{ easing:"easeOutQuint",  duration: 1000,

            step: function(now, fx){
                //at each step we can adjust the scale
                to make it look smaller
        if (fx.prop == "opacity" && fx.pos>=0.1) {
            //work out the amount to scale
            var xx = 0.5/(fx.pos);
            //apply the scale
            $(this).css('transform','scale('+xx+')');
        }
        }, complete: function () {
        }//end of second complete function
        });//end of second animation
    }//end of first complete function
});  //end of first animation

}
```

Save and close this file.

In the code above we have written
$(this).delay(150).animate({

This normally would have been written as

$(this).animate({

As the name suggests, however, we have applied a delay before calling
this function. The jQuery function sets a timer to delay the execution of
items in its queue. It accepts an integer as a parameter, indicating the
number of milliseconds to delay execution. So in our case, we asked for the
code to wait 150 milliseconds before executing our animate function.

I would like to add that this `delay()` method is best for only certain game engines where you are delaying between queued jQuery effects. It doesn't offer a way to cancel the delay; therefore, in certain cases, `delay()` is not a replacement for JavaScript's native `setTimeout` function, which may be more appropriate.

Next, we need to call our new function. Open the `SZ_zombie_movement.js` file in the `js` folder. Carefully modify some old lines and type the following new lines (all modified and new text is in bold):

```
//let's create a zombie
function SZ_createZombie(whichOne){

//create a new div to hold the zombie SS
  var div = document.createElement('div');
//and another for the bubble zombie SS
  var div2 = document.createElement('div');

//we need to hard code the CSS styles we want
  div.setAttribute('style','position: fixed; top:0; left:0;')
//and the same for our bubble zombie
  div2.setAttribute('style','position: fixed; top:0; left:0;')

//we want to position our zombie exactly at the tip of the planet
  var top_position= $('#SZ0_0').height() * 0.435;

//Xpos can be anywhere on our x axis
  var left_position = Math.floor(Math.random() * ($('#SZ0_0').
  width())-(ratio*50)) + (ratio*50);

//record this left position
  leftx_zombie[whichOne-1]=left_position;

//let's position our zombie
  div.style.left = left_position+'px'; div.style.top = top_
  position+'px';
```

```
//and the same for our bubble zombie
  div2.style.left = left_position+'px'; div2.style.top = top_
  position+'px';

//give it an id
  div.id = 'zombie'+whichOne;
//also for our bubble zombie
  div2.id = 'bubble_zombie'+whichOne;

//finally let's add our zombie to the screen
  document.body.appendChild(div);
//finally add in our bubble zombie to the screen too
  document.body.appendChild(div2);

//put this new zombie through our SS function
 setup_zombie_SS(whichOne);

//put this new zombie through our animate function
  SZ_animateZombie(whichOne);

//hide the bubble zombies at the start
  $("#bubble_zombie"+whichOne).css('transform','scale('+0+')');

//bind the users mouse click to this zombie
$("#zombie"+whichOne).bind('mousedown touchstart', function (e) {
    //make sure the zombie is currently walking
    if($("#zombie"+whichOne).css('opacity') != 0) {
        //first we want to fire the gun
         fireGun(event);
        //acknowledge the hit
         zombieHit(whichOne-1);
    }
  });
}
```

```
//we need to keep track of the current scale values
 var scalex_zombie =  [0,0,0,0,0,0];
//we also need to keep track of the left position
 var leftx_zombie =  [0,0,0,0,0,0];

//let's animate our zombie towards us
function SZ_animateZombie(whichOne){

     //assign the speed for each of our zombies
     var timex =  [13000,8000,16000,14000,10000,18000];

     //assign a user friendly name for our div
     var $zombiex = $("#zombie"+whichOne);

     //reset the zombies scale value
     $zombiex.css('transform','scale('+0+')');

     //reset the zombies opacity
     $zombiex.css({opacity:1});

     //work out the amount the zombie has to come towards us
     var amty =  ($(window).height()*0.7);// -($zombiex.
     height()*2));//topx);

     //each type of zombie will have their own walking style
     var ZS_ease = ['easeInSine','easeOutQuart','easeInOutQuad',
     'easeInSine','easeOutQuart','easeInOutQuad'];

     //finally we are ready to animate
       $zombiex.delay(timex[whichOne-1]/3).animate({
             //first bring our zombie slowly down the screen
                 left:    "+="+0.001+ "px",
       },{ easing:ZS_ease[whichOne-1],  duration:
       timex[whichOne-1],

           step: function(now, fx){
             //at each step we can manipulate the scale of
             our zombie
```

141

```
            if (fx.prop == "left") {
                //work out the amount to scale
                var xx = (fx.pos)*16;
            //do a check to see if we should end this
            animation
                    if(xx>15){
                        //stop all animation
                        // $(this).stop();
                        //call a function to reset this zombie
                        SZ_resetZombie(whichOne,0);
                    } else {
                        //apply the scale
                        $(this).css('transform',
                        'scale('+xx+')');
                        //record this new scale value
                        scalex_zombie[whichOne-1]=xx;
                    }
                }
            }, complete: function () {
                }
            });
}
//a function to completely reset our zombie
function SZ_resetZombie(whichOne, zombieBubble_generate){

    //reset this zombies hit counter
    zombieHits_counter[whichOne-1]=0;

    //assign a user friendly name for our div
    var $zombiex = $("#zombie"+whichOne);

    //we need to stop this zombies animations
    $zombiex.stop();
```

```
//we want to position our zombie exactly at the tip of the
planet
 var top_position= $('#SZO_O').height() * 0.435;

//should we generate a bubble zombie?
  if(zombieBubble_generate==1){
    //assign a user friendly name for our bubble zombie div
    var $bubble_zombiex = $("#bubble_zombie"+whichOne);
    //let's re-position our bubble zombie to our stored
    value
    $bubble_zombiex.css({top: top_position+'px',left:
    $zombiex.css("left"), opacity:1});
    //apply the scale
    $bubble_zombiex.css('transform','scale('+scalex_
    zombie[whichOne-1]+')');
    //call our bubble zombie animation function
    bubbleZombie_flyAway(whichOne);
  }

//Xpos can be anywhere on our x axis
 var left_position = Math.floor(Math.random() *
 ($('#SZO_O').width())-(ratio*50)) + (ratio*50);

//record this left position
 leftx_zombie[whichOne-1]=left_position;

//let's re-position our zombie
$zombiex.css({top: top_position+'px', left: left_
position+'px', opacity:0});

//finally let's make the zombie come towards the screen
again
 //SZ_animateZombie(whichOne);
}
```

You can now save and close this file. We are now ready to test our code. Go back to the My_Work_Files folder and double-click the default.html file. You should now see the bubble zombies animate upward and then away into the distance.

Again, please note that you may notice that the zombies may stop coming all together. This was done on purpose for some code that we will write later. For now, just refresh your browser (press F5) and the game should restart.

Next, we will only allow a certain number of shots from our gun before it needs to be reloaded.

Did the code not work? First, check to see that you have modified the SZ_resetZombie function to include an extra parameter (the code in red):

```
$bubble_zombiex.css({top: top_position+'px',left: $zombiex.
css("left"), opacity:1});
```

and

```
$zombiex.css({top: top_position+'px', left: left_position+'px',
opacity:0});
```

Also, the tail end of the code in the SZ_movement.js file has a few repetitive characters. Please make sure that they are all written as shown here:

```
            }
        }, complete: function () {
        }//end of second complete function
        });//end of second animation
```

```
}//end of first complete function
}); //end of first animation
```

If the code is still not working, then please do not hesitate to message me on Twitter @zarrarchishti.

What caused the bubble zombie to bounce upward?

You learned about *easing functions* in Chapter 6. As a reminder, an easing function specifies a zombie's rate of change over time. So in our case, we want to make the bubble zombie go upward and bounce, so we used `easeOutElastic:`.

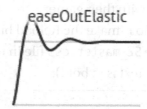

What is opacity?

The `opacity` property sets or returns the transparency level of an element. This is where 1 is not transparent at all, 0.5 is 50% see-through, and 0 is completely transparent.

What is happening after the bubble zombie flies off?

It is important to note that the first thing that we do is perform the following check:

```
if (fx.prop == "opacity" && fx.pos>=0.1) {
```

145

The && means logical AND (i.e., if the fx property is opacity AND the fx position is greater than or equal to 0.1).

The reason we needed to place this check for the position is because the first value is almost always 0. If we allowed this, then we would be dividing by zero, which, of course, is undefined. This would lead to problems and indeterminable behavior.

Finally, we take this value and place it as a scale value for the bubble zombie. Over time, this makes the bubble zombie appear smaller, thus giving it the impression of disappearing into the distance.

Reloading the Gun

You may have noticed that our Reload button is pretty redundant so far. Of course, it does cause our gun to animate despite playing no part in our game. So far, the ultimate aim is to give the user a fixed amount of shots before the gun stops shooting. At this time, the Reload button prompts the user to press it to continue with their game.

The first thing we will do is make the Reload button invisible at the start of the game. Open the SZ_master.css file in our CSS folder. Type the following new line (all new text is in bold):

```
html {

    height: 100%;

}
body {
    padding: 0 0 0 0;
    margin: 0;
    user-select: none;
    cursor: crosshair;
}
img {
    max-width: 100%;
```

146

```
        height: auto;
        user-drag: none;
        user-select: none;
        -moz-user-select: none;
        -webkit-user-drag: none;
        -webkit-user-select: none;
        -ms-user-select: none;
    }
#SZ0_0 {
        position: fixed;
        top: 0;
        left: 0;
        min-width: 100%;
        min-height: 100%;
    }
 #SZ0_1 {
        position: fixed;
        bottom: 0;
        right: 0;
}
 #SZ0_2 {
        position: fixed;
        top: 0;
        left: 0;
        cursor: pointer;
      opacity:0;
}
 #SZ0_3 {
        position: fixed;
        top: 0;
        right: 0;
}
```

Save and close this file.

In Chapter 3, I suggested that you group these three divs (i.e., #SZ0_1, #SZ0_2, #SZ0_3) together since they shared the same properties. However, how would we be able to add a new property just for #SZ0_2? We would do this with the following code:

```
#SZ0_1, #SZ0_2, #SZ0_3 {
      position: fixed;
      top: 0;
      right: 0;
}
#SZ0_2 {
opacity:0;
}
```

Anything written with the extra #SZ0_2 code appends whatever is already coded for it.

Go back to the My_Work_Files folder and double-click the default. html file. The Reload button should have disappeared. If you try to click it, however, it still shoots. So we need to place a check to make sure that we only perform the gun animation when the Reload button is visible. Also, it's a good time to place a maximum number of shots on the gun.

Open the SZ_zombie_movement.js file and type the following modified line (all modified text is in red):

```
//let's create a zombie
function SZ_createZombie(whichOne){

 //create a new div to hold the zombie SS
   var div = document.createElement('div');
 //and another for the bubble zombie SS
   var div2 = document.createElement('div');
```

```
//we need to hard code the CSS styles we want
  div.setAttribute('style','position: fixed; top:0; left:0;')
//and the same for our bubble zombie
  div2.setAttribute('style','position: fixed; top:0; left:0;')

//we want to position our zombie exactly at the tip of the
planet
  var top_position= $('#SZO_0').height() * 0.435;

//Xpos can be anywhere on our x axis
  var left_position = Math.floor(Math.random() * ($('#SZO_0').
  width())-(ratio*50)) + (ratio*50);

//record this left position
  leftx_zombie[whichOne-1]=left_position;

//let's position our zombie
  div.style.left = left_position+'px'; div.style.top = top_
  position+'px';
//and the same for our bubble zombie
  div2.style.left = left_position+'px'; div2.style.top =
  top_position+'px';

//give it an id
  div.id = 'zombie'+whichOne;
//also for our bubble zombie
  div2.id = 'bubble_zombie'+whichOne;

//finally let's add our zombie to the screen
  document.body.appendChild(div);
//finally add in our bubble zombie to the screen too
  document.body.appendChild(div2);

//put this new zombie through our SS function
 setup_zombie_SS(whichOne);
```

149

```
//put this new zombie through our animate function
  SZ_animateZombie(whichOne);

//hide the bubble zombies at the start
  $("#bubble_zombie"+whichOne).css('transform','scale('+0+')');

//bind the users mouse click to this zombie
$("#zombie"+whichOne).bind('mousedown touchstart', function (e) {
  //make sure the zombie is currently walking
    if($("#zombie"+whichOne).css('opacity') != 0 &&
    $("#SZ0_2").css('opacity') != 1) {
        //first we want to fire the gun
          fireGun(event);
        //acknowledge the hit
          zombieHit(whichOne-1);
      }
    });

}


//we need to keep track of the current scale values
 var scalex_zombie =  [0,0,0,0,0,0];
//we also need to keep track of the left position
 var leftx_zombie =  [0,0,0,0,0,0];

//let's animate our zombie towards us
function SZ_animateZombie(whichOne){

    //assign the speed for each of our zombies
    var timex =  [13000,8000,16000,14000,10000,18000];

    //assign a user friendly name for our div
    var $zombiex = $("#zombie"+whichOne);

    //reset the zombies scale value
      $zombiex.css('transform','scale('+0+')');
```

```
//reset the zombies opacity
$zombiex.css({opacity:1});

//work out the amount the zombie has to come towards us
var amty =  ($(window).height()*0.7);// -($zombiex.
height()*2));//topx);

//each type of zombie will have their own walking style
var ZS_ease = ['easeInSine','easeOutQuart','easeInOutQuad',
'easeInSine','easeOutQuart','easeInOutQuad'];

//finally we are ready to animate
  $zombiex.delay(timex[whichOne-1]/3).animate({
          //first bring our zombie slowly down the screen
              left:    "+="+0.001+ "px",
      },{ easing:ZS_ease[whichOne-1],  duration:
      timex[whichOne-1],

          step: function(now, fx){
          //at each step we can manipulate the scale of
          our zombie
            if (fx.prop == "left") {
                //work out the amount to scale
                var xx = (fx.pos)*16;
            //do a check to see if we should end this
            animation
                  if(xx>15){
                      //stop all animation
                          // $(this).stop();
                      //call a function to reset this zombie
                      SZ_resetZombie(whichOne,0);
                    } else {
                      //apply the scale
                      $(this).css('transform',
                      'scale('+xx+')');
```

```
                          //record this new scale value
                          scalex_zombie[whichOne-1]=xx;
                      }
                  }
          }, complete: function () {
              }
        });
}
//a function to completely reset our zombie
function SZ_resetZombie(whichOne, zombieBubble_generate){

    //reset this zombies hit counter
     zombieHits_counter[whichOne-1]=0;

    //assign a user friendly name for our div
     var $zombiex = $("#zombie"+whichOne);

    //we need to stop this zombies animations
     $zombiex.stop();

    //we want to position our zombie exactly at the tip of the
    planet
     var top_position= $('#SZ0_0').height() * 0.435;

    //should we generate a bubble zombie?
     if(zombieBubble_generate==1){
        //assign a user friendly name for our bubble zombie div
         var $bubble_zombiex = $("#bubble_zombie"+whichOne);
        //let's re-position our bubble zombie to our stored
        value
         $bubble_zombiex.css({top: top_position+'px',left:
         $zombiex.css("left"), opacity:1});
        //apply the scale
         $bubble_zombiex.css('transform',
         'scale('+scalex_zombie[whichOne-1]+')');
```

```
    //call our bubble zombie animation function
    bubbleZombie_flyAway(whichOne);
  }

  //Xpos can be anywhere on our x axis
  var left_position = Math.floor(Math.random() *
  ($('#SZO_0').width())-(ratio*50)) + (ratio*50);

  //record this left position
  leftx_zombie[whichOne-1]=left_position;

  //let's re-position our zombie
  $zombiex.css({top: top_position+'px',
  left: left_position+'px', opacity:0});

  //finally let's make the zombie come towards the screen
  again
  //SZ_animateZombie(whichOne);
}
```

You can now save and close this file.

Here we are basing our decision on the opacity of various elements. We will continue to do so in the next section of code as well. It would be a good idea to place these checks in a separate function, and then simply call that function in the code that requires it.

Next, we need to ensure that we show and hide our Reload button at the appropriate times. Open the SZ_touch.js file and type the following new and modified lines (all new text is in bold):

```
//We need a flag to keep track to avoid repetition of
animations before the first has finished
var canIclick= 0;

//this function is called to reload our gun
function reloadGun(e) {
```

```
//Let's check if we can allow this to occur
   if(canIclick== 0 && $("#SZO_2").css('opacity') == 1){
     //looks like we can so we better set our flag
       canIclick=1;
       $("#SZO_1").animateSprite("play", "reload");
     //reset the current shots
       current_shots=0;
     //hide the reload button
       $("#SZO_2").css({opacity:0});
   }
}

//place a maximum number of shots
var max_shots=5;
//keep track of current number of shots
var current_shots=0;

//this function is called to fire our gun
function fireGun(e) {
 //Let's check if we can allow this to occur
   if(canIclick== 0 && $("#SZO_2").css('opacity') != 1){
     //looks like we can so we better set our flag
       canIclick=1;
       $("#SZO_1").animateSprite("play", "fire");
     //increment our shots
       current_shots++;
     //check to see if we have reached the maximum
       if(current_shots>=max_shots){
         //show the reload button
           $("#SZO_2").css({opacity:1});
       }//if
   }
}
```

```
//array to keep track of the zombie hits
 var zombieHits_counter = [0,0,0,0,0,0];
//array for each zombies limit
 var zombieHits_limits = [2,1,3,2,1,3];

//this function will keep track of the zombie hits and act
accordingly
function zombieHit(whichOne){

 //increment the counter
  zombieHits_counter[whichOne]++;

 //check to see if this zombie has reached its limit
  if(zombieHits_counter[whichOne] >= zombieHits_
limits[whichOne]){
    //reset this zombie
     SZ_resetZombie(whichOne+1,1);
  }
}
```

You can now save and close this file.

Go back to the My_Work_Files folder and double-click the default.
html file. You should see that the gun needs to be reloaded after firing
five times. By pressing the Reload button, two things happen: the Reload
button disappears and you are able to fire the gun again.

Next, we solve a few problematic areas that have arisen in our game.

Further Information

How does the code know when to fire and reload the gun?

This is a good question and I would like to point out that the code you
have just entered is probably one of the more complex and interesting we
have written to date. There are two steps to determining the answer to this
question: (1) check and set the opacity of the Reload button, and (2) check
the number of shots fired against the maximum allowed. So let's take a
closer look at what we wrote.

You will have noticed we deal a lot with *opacity*; for instance, the first
portion of code we wrote was

```
opacity:0;
```

As you discovered earlier in the previous section, opacity is essentially
the object's level of transparency. In this case, the object is SZO_2, which is
the Reload button image.

At the start, we set the opacity of the Reload button to 0. From this
point onward, all we have to do is check the opacity of this button before
proceeding. This is done by using the following check:

```
$("#SZO_2").css('opacity') != 1
```

!= means "not equal to"

By using this check, we can tell the code to fire the gun or show the
Reload button.

Once the Reload button is pressed, we can hide it, thus allowing the
gun to be fired again.

One final thought. When do we stop allowing the gun to be fired? The
following code sets the maximum number of shots that can be fired before
reloading:

```
var max_shots=5;
```

We also need to keep track of the current number of shots fired. We do
this using the following variable:

```
var current_shots=0;
```

Now every time a shot is fired, we can compare the two variables, as follows:

```
if(current_shots>=max_shots){
```

If this is true, we stop any further shots and force the user to reload their gun.

Clean up the Depths and Click Zones

You may have noticed that there are some areas of the planet's surface that do not result in a gun fire when clicked. The reason for this is because you are clicking a zombie or a bubble zombie that is invisible (i.e., not in use). But, our current code does not allow the gun to be fired.

Part 1: Ensuring Gun Fire

Open the SZ_zombie_movement.js file and type the following new lines (all new text is in bold) and some modified lines (all in red):

```
//let's create a zombie
function SZ_createZombie(whichOne){

//create a new div to hold the zombie SS
  var div = document.createElement('div');
//and another for the bubble zombie SS
  var div2 = document.createElement('div');

//we need to hard code the CSS styles we want
  div.setAttribute('style','position: fixed; top:0; left:0;')
//and the same for our bubble zombie
  div2.setAttribute('style','position: fixed; top:0; left:0;')

//we want to position our zombie exactly at the tip of the planet
  var top_position= $('#SZO_0').height() * 0.435;
```

157

```
//Xpos can be anywhere on our x axis
  var left_position = Math.floor(Math.random() * ($('#SZO_O').
  width())-(ratio*50)) + (ratio*50);

//record this left position
  leftx_zombie[whichOne-1]=left_position;

//let's position our zombie
  div.style.left = left_position+'px'; div.style.top =
  top_position+'px';
//and the same for our bubble zombie
  div2.style.left = left_position+'px'; div2.style.top =
  top_position+'px';

//give it an id
  div.id = 'zombie'+whichOne;
//also for our bubble zombie
  div2.id = 'bubble_zombie'+whichOne;

//finally let's add our zombie to the screen
  document.body.appendChild(div);
//finally add in our bubble zombie to the screen too
  document.body.appendChild(div2);

//put this new zombie through our SS function
 setup_zombie_SS(whichOne);

//put this new zombie through our animate function
  SZ_animateZombie(whichOne);

//hide the bubble zombies at the start
  $("#bubble_zombie"+whichOne).css('transform',
  'scale('+0+')');

//bind the users mouse click to this zombie
$("#zombie"+whichOne).bind('mousedown touchstart', function (e) {
```

```
    //make sure the reload button is showing
    if($("#SZ0_2").css('opacity') != 1) {
        //first we want to fire the gun
        fireGun(event);
        //acknowledge the hit
if($("#zombie"+whichOne).css('opacity') != 0){
        zombieHit(whichOne-1);
}
    }
});
//bind the users mouse click to the bubble zombie
$("#bubble_zombie"+whichOne).bind('mousedown touchstart',
function (e) {
    //make sure the reload button is showing
    if($("#SZ0_2").css('opacity') != 1) {
        //first we want to fire the gun
        fireGun(event);
    }
});
}

//we need to keep track of the current scale values
var scalex_zombie = [0,0,0,0,0,0];
//we also need to keep track of the left position
var leftx_zombie = [0,0,0,0,0,0];

//let's animate our zombie towards us
function SZ_animateZombie(whichOne){

    //assign the speed for each of our zombies
    var timex = [13000,8000,16000,14000,10000,18000];

    //assign a user friendly name for our div
```

```
var $zombiex = $("#zombie"+whichOne);

//reset the zombies scale value
$zombiex.css('transform','scale('+0+')');

//reset the zombies opacity
$zombiex.css({opacity:1});

//work out the amount the zombie has to come towards us
var amty =  ($(window).height()*0.7);// -($zombiex.
height()*2));//topx);

//each type of zombie will have their own walking style
var ZS_ease = ['easeInSine','easeOutQuart','easeInOutQuad',
'easeInSine','easeOutQuart','easeInOutQuad'];

//finally we are ready to animate
   $zombiex.delay(timex[whichOne-1]/3).animate({
            //first bring our zombie slowly down the screen
            left:   "+="+0.001+ "px",
      },{ easing:ZS_ease[whichOne-1],  duration:
      timex[whichOne-1],

         step: function(now, fx){
            //at each step we can manipulate the scale of
            our zombie
            if (fx.prop == "left") {
               //work out the amount to scale
               var xx = (fx.pos)*16;
            //do a check to see if we should end this
            animation
                  if(xx>15){
                     //stop all animation
                     // $(this).stop();
                        //call a function to reset this zombie
```

```
                        SZ_resetZombie(whichOne,0);
                    } else {
                        //apply the scale
                        $(this).css('transform',
                        'scale('+xx+')');
                        //record this new scale value
                        scalex_zombie[whichOne-1]=xx;
                    }
                }
            }, complete: function () {
                }
        });
}
//a function to completely reset our zombie
function SZ_resetZombie(whichOne, zombieBubble_generate){

    //reset this zombies hit counter
    zombieHits_counter[whichOne-1]=0;

    //assign a user friendly name for our div
    var $zombiex = $("#zombie"+whichOne);

    //we need to stop this zombies animations
    $zombiex.stop();

    //we want to position our zombie exactly at the tip of the
    planet
    var top_position= $('#SZ0_0').height() * 0.435;

    //should we generate a bubble zombie?
    if(zombieBubble_generate==1){
        //assign a user friendly name for our bubble zombie div
        var $bubble_zombiex = $("#bubble_zombie"+whichOne);
        //let's re-position our bubble zombie to our stored value
```

```
        $bubble_zombiex.css({top: top_position+'px',left:
        $zombiex.css("left"), opacity:1});
      //apply the scale
      $bubble_zombiex.css('transform',
      'scale('+scalex_zombie[whichOne-1]+')');
      //call our bubble zombie animation function
      bubbleZombie_flyAway(whichOne);
    }

  //Xpos can be anywhere on our x axis
  var left_position = Math.floor(Math.random() *
  ($('#SZO_0').width())-(ratio*50)) + (ratio*50);

  //record this left position
  leftx_zombie[whichOne-1]=left_position;

  //let's re-position our zombie
  $zombiex.css({top: top_position+'px', left:
  left_position+'px', opacity:0});

  //finally let's make the zombie come towards the screen
  again
  //SZ_animateZombie(whichOne);
}
```

You can now save and close this file.

I want to explain the preceding red code. Originally, the line of code was

```
if($("#zombie"+whichOne).css('opacity') != 0 && $("#SZO_2").
css('opacity') != 1) {
```

However, we removed the first part of the if statement and placed it further down. This is because we need to ensure that the Reload button is visible, regardless of the zombie's div.

Go back to the My_Work_Files folder and double-click the default.html file. You should see that the gun can fire anywhere on the planet surface.

Next, we look at the zombie depth levels.

Part 2: Zombie Depth Levels

Another issue that you may have noticed is that sometimes one zombie appears to walk over another, such as in the following screenshot of the current game:

What is happening here is that the female zombie is of a lower depth; however, because she is faster in this case, she appears on top of the slower zombie. To counter this, we need to continually check and adjust the depths while the game is being played. Also, we always want our gun to be above the zombies.

Open the SZ_zombie_movement.js file and type the following new lines (all new text is in bold) and some modified lines (all in red):

```
//let's create a zombie
function SZ_createZombie(whichOne){

 //create a new div to hold the zombie SS
   var div = document.createElement('div');
 //and another for the bubble zombie SS
   var div2 = document.createElement('div');

 //we need to hard code the CSS styles we want
   div.setAttribute('style','position: fixed; top:0; left:0;')
 //and the same for our bubble zombie
   div2.setAttribute('style','position: fixed; top:0; left:0;')

 //we want to position our zombie exactly at the tip of the
planet
   var top_position= $('#SZO_0').height() * 0.435;

 //Xpos can be anywhere on our x axis
   var left_position = Math.floor(Math.random() * ($('#SZO_0').
   width())-(ratio*50)) + (ratio*50);

 //record this left position
   leftx_zombie[whichOne-1]=left_position;

 //let's position our zombie
   div.style.left = left_position+'px'; div.style.top =
   top_position+'px';
 //and the same for our bubble zombie
   div2.style.left = left_position+'px'; div2.style.top =
   top_position+'px';

 //give it an id
   div.id = 'zombie'+whichOne;
 //also for our bubble zombie
   div2.id = 'bubble_zombie'+whichOne;
```

```
//finally let's add our zombie to the screen
  document.body.appendChild(div);
//finally add in our bubble zombie to the screen too
  document.body.appendChild(div2);

//put this new zombie through our SS function
 setup_zombie_SS(whichOne);

//put this new zombie through our animate function
  SZ_animateZombie(whichOne);

//hide the bubble zombies at the start
  $("#bubble_zombie"+whichOne).css('transform','scale('+0+')');

 //set the zindex for the zombie
 $("#zombie"+whichOne).css("z-index", whichOne+100);
 //set the zindex for the bubble zombie
 $("#bubble_zombie"+whichOne).css("z-index", whichOne);
//ensure the zindex for the gun is the highest
 $("#SZ0_1").css("z-index", 200);

//bind the users mouse click to this zombie
$("#zombie"+whichOne).bind('mousedown touchstart', function (e) {
   //make sure the reload button is showing
    if($("#SZ0_2").css('opacity') != 1) {
        //first we want to fire the gun
         fireGun(event);
        //acknowledge the hit
if($("#zombie"+whichOne).css('opacity') != 0){
        zombieHit(whichOne-1);
}
    }
  });
```

```
//bind the users mouse click to the bubble zombie
 $("#bubble_zombie"+whichOne).bind('mousedown touchstart',
function (e) {
   //make sure the reload button is showing
    if($("#SZ0_2").css('opacity') != 1) {
        //first we want to fire the gun
          fireGun(event);

      }
    });

}

//we need to keep track of the current scale values
 var scalex_zombie =  [0,0,0,0,0,0];
//we also need to keep track of the left position
 var leftx_zombie =  [0,0,0,0,0,0];
//let's animate our zombie towards us
function SZ_animateZombie(whichOne){
    //assign the speed for each of our zombies
    var timex =  [13000,8000,16000,14000,10000,18000];

    //assign a user friendly name for our div
    var $zombiex = $("#zombie"+whichOne);

    //reset the zombies scale value
     $zombiex.css('transform','scale('+0+')');

    //reset the zombies opacity
     $zombiex.css({opacity:1});

    //work out the amount the zombie has to come towards us
    var amty =  ($(window).height()*0.7);// -($zombiex.
    height()*2));//topx);
```

```javascript
//each type of zombie will have their own walking style
var ZS_ease = ['easeInSine','easeOutQuart','easeInOutQuad',
'easeInSine','easeOutQuart','easeInOutQuad'];

//finally we are ready to animate
  $zombiex.delay(timex[whichOne-1]/3).animate({
          //first bring our zombie slowly down the screen
          left:   "+="+0.001+ "px",
    },{ easing:ZS_ease[whichOne-1],  duration:
    timex[whichOne-1],

        step: function(now, fx){
          //at each step we can manipulate the scale of
          our zombie
          if (fx.prop == "left") {
              //work out the amount to scale
              var xx = (fx.pos)*16;
            //do a check to see if we should end this
            animation
                  if(xx>15){
                    //stop all animation
                    // $(this).stop();
                    //call a function to reset this zombie
                    SZ_resetZombie(whichOne,0);
                  } else {
                    //apply the scale
                    $(this).css('transform',
                    'scale('+xx+')');
                    //record this new scale value
                    scalex_zombie[whichOne-1]=xx;
                    //check the depth levels
                    var i = 0;
                    while (i < 6) {
```

```
                        //check to see if the scale is
                        bigger
                          if(scalex_zombie[whichOne-1]
                          >scalex_zombie[i] && ($(this).
                          zIndex() < $("#zombie"+(i+1)).
                          zIndex()) &&
                          scalex_zombie[i]!=0){
                          var i_index =
                          $("#zombie"+(i+1)).zIndex();
                          //change the i one first
                          $("#zombie"+(i+1)).css("z-index",
                          $(this).css( "z-index" ));
                          //now change this one
                          $(this).css("z-index", i_index);
                          } //end of if
                        i++;
                      }//end of while loop
                  }
              }
          }, complete: function () {
              }
        });
}
//need to keep track of the current zindex for zombies
var zindex_current=0;
//a function to completely reset our zombie
function SZ_resetZombie(whichOne, zombieBubble_generate){

    //reset this zombies hit counter
    zombieHits_counter[whichOne-1]=0;

    //assign a user friendly name for our div
    var $zombiex = $("#zombie"+whichOne);
```

168

```
//we need to stop this zombies animations
 $zombiex.stop();
```

```
//we want to position our zombie exactly at the tip of the
planet
 var top_position= $('#SZ0_0').height() * 0.435;
```

```
//should we generate a bubble zombie?
 if(zombieBubble_generate==1){
    //assign a user friendly name for our bubble zombie div
     var $bubble_zombiex = $("#bubble_zombie"+whichOne);
    //let's re-position our bubble zombie to our stored
    value
     $bubble_zombiex.css({top: top_position+'px',left:
     $zombiex.css("left"), opacity:1});
    //apply the scale
     $bubble_zombiex.css('transform',
     'scale('+scalex_zombie[whichOne-1]+')');
    //call our bubble zombie animation function
     bubbleZombie_flyAway(whichOne);
 }
//Xpos can be anywhere on our x axis
 var left_position = Math.floor(Math.random() *
 ($('#SZ0_0').width())-(ratio*50)) + (ratio*50);
```

```
//record this left position
 leftx_zombie[whichOne-1]=left_position;
```

```
//let's re-position our zombie
 $zombiex.css({top: top_position+'px', left: left_
 position+'px', opacity:0});
```

```
//set the zindex for the zombie
 zindex_current++;
```

```
$("#zombie"+whichOne).css("z-index", zindex_current);

    //finally let's make the zombie come towards the screen
    again
    //SZ_animateZombie(whichOne);
}
```

You can now save and close this file.

Go back to the My_Work_Files folder and double-click the default.html file. You should see that the zombies do not overlap each other as they did before. Also, the gun should always appear above the zombies.

Next, we look at creating a Game Over screen.

What exactly is a z-index?

The z-index is the order of each element. Imagine that all of our elements, such as the gun image or the score image, are lined up like a pack of cards. If you slightly spread the cards, you see the top card fully while the ones underneath are only slightly visible. This is because when cards overlap, the visibility of one particular card depends on its location from the top.

In the same way, when our elements overlap each other, their visibility depends on their stack order or z-index. So an element with a bigger z-index will be more visible when overlapped with an element of a lower z-index.

This really becomes useful when our zombies, which are continuously randomly placed, start to overlap each other. JavaScript allows us to manipulate the z-indices, and therefore we can program the elements to reorder to ensure that elements that are further away from us are kept behind those elements that are closer.

What is happening in the following line of code that we just wrote?

```
while (i < 6) {
```

This is an example of the while loop. Almost all programming languages have a while loop, which essentially allows code to be executed repeatedly, depending on the conditions placed.

So in our case, the code inside the while loop executes continuously until the i variable is no longer less than six.

Intro Splash and "Game Over" Screens

So far, our game starts immediately and does not really end. It would be nice to have both an intro screen and a Game Over screen.

Part 1: Images Folder

Go to the images folder in the Raw Images folder of the My_Work_Files folder. Locate the files named splash_intro.png and splash_gameover. png, and copy them to the Images folder, which should now look like the following screenshot:

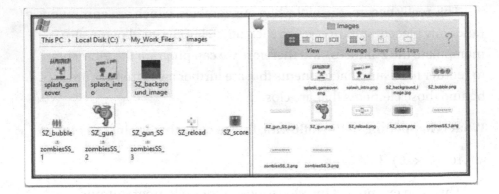

Part 2: Stopping and Starting

To stop and start the game for the intro splash screen and the Game Over screen, we need to add a lot of new code and perform changes to existing code. Please pay close attention to the new lines (in bold) and the modified lines (in red).

Nearly all of our existing files will need to be modified. So let's start by opening the default.html file and type the following new lines (all new text is in bold):

```html
<html>
 <head>
  <script src="js/jquery.js"></script>
  <script src="js/jquery-ui.js"></script>
  <script src="js/SZ_main.js"></script>
  <script src="js/SZ_setupContent.js"></script>
  <script src="js/SZ_movement.js"></script>
  <script src="js/ss.js"></script>
  <script src="js/SZ_SS.js"></script>
  <script src="js/SZ_touch.js"></script>
  <script src="js/SZ_zombie_movement.js"></script>
```

```
<link href="css/SZ_master.css" rel="stylesheet" />
</head>
<body>
 <div id="SZ_maincontent">
   <img id="SZ0_0" src="images/SZ_background_image.jpg"
   onmousemove="rotateGun(event)"  onmousedown="fireGun(event)" />
   <div id="SZO_1" ></div>
   <div id="SZO_2" >
    <img  src="images/SZ_reload.png"
    onmousedown="reloadGun(event)" />
   </div>
   <div id="SZO_3" >
    <img src="images/SZ_score.png" />
   </div>
   <div id="SZO_4" onmousedown="start_game();"/>
  </div>
 </body>
</html>
```

Save the file and then close it.

Open the SZ_master.css file and type the following new lines (all new text is in bold):

```
html {
     height: 100%;
     }

body {
     padding: 0 0 0 0;
     margin: 0;
     user-select: none;
     cursor: crosshair;
     }
```

```css
img  {
        max-width: 100%;
        height: auto;
        user-drag: none;
        user-select: none;
        -moz-user-select: none;
        -webkit-user-drag: none;
        -webkit-user-select: none;
        -ms-user-select: none;
     }
#SZO_0 {
         position: fixed;
         top: 0;
         left: 0;
         min-width: 100%;
         min-height: 100%;
        }
 #SZO_1 {
         position: fixed;
         bottom: 0;
         right: 0;
      opacity:0;
}
 #SZO_2 {
         position: fixed;
         top: 0;
         left: 0;
         cursor: pointer;
      opacity:0;
}
```

```
#SZO_3 {
        position: fixed;
        top: 0;
        right: 0;
        opacity:0;
}
#SZO_4 {
        position: fixed;
        cursor: pointer;
        background-size:cover;
        opacity:0;
}
```

Save the file and then close it.

Open the SZ_setupContent.js file and type the following new lines (all new text is in bold):

```
//we will need a new ratio var
var ratio_use = ratio;
//main function
function main_call_setupContent() {
  //need to resize all elements
  //first we set their normal sizes in CSS

  //Gun
  $('#SZO_1').css('width', 150 * ratio);
  $('#SZO_1').css('height', 150 * ratio);

  //Reload Button
  $('#SZO_2').css('width', 200 * ratio);
  $('#SZO_2').css('height', 90 * ratio);
```

```
//Score
 $('#SZ0_3').css('width', 235 * ratio);
 $('#SZ0_3').css('height', 100 * ratio);

 //Intro and Game over
 if($(window).height()<$(window).width()){
  //work out a ratio based on height
  ratio_use =  $(window).height()/800;
 }//end if
 //apply this new ratio to our intro/game over
 $('#SZ0_4').css('width', 868 * ratio_use);
 $('#SZ0_4').css('height', 701 * ratio_use);
 $('#SZ0_4').css('left', ($(window).width()/2)-
((868 * ratio_use)/2));
 //make sure it is half way
 $('#SZ0_4').css('top', ($(window).height()/2)-
((701 * ratio_use)/2));

 //Any sprite sheets?
   //Our Gun
     setup_gun_SS();

//Create all our 6 zombies
 for (i = 1; i < 7; i++) {
  //this will get called 6 times
  SZ_createZombie(i);
  }
 //call the intro
  start_end_game(0);
}

var gameEnded=0;
//Intro or Game Over of game
 function start_end_game(whichOne) {
```

```
//hide the elements
for (i = 1; i < 4; i++) {
 //this will get called 3 times
 $('#SZO_'+i).css({opacity:0});
}//for

//hide the zombies
for (i = 1; i < 7; i++) {
//we need to stop this zombies animations
 $('#zombie_'+i).stop();
 $('#zombie_'+i).css({opacity:0});
 $('#bubble_zombie_'+i).css({opacity:0});
}//for
if(whichOne==0){
 //START OF GAME
//change the background image
 $('#SZO_4').css('background-image', 'url(images/
 splash_intro.png)');
} else {
 //GAME OVER
//show the score
 $('#SZO_3').css({opacity:1});
//change the background image
 $('#SZO_4').css('background-image',
 'url(images/splash_gameover.png)');
}
//make sure it is half way
 $('#SZO_4').css('top', ($(window).height()/2)-
 ((701 * ratio_use)/2));
   //finally show the intro or game over image
    $('#SZO_4').css({opacity:1});
//stop the user from firing
```

```
            gameEnded= 1;
}//end of function
//start the game
  function start_game() {
        //reset the zindex
         zindex_current=0;

        //reload the gun
         current_shots=0;
        //allow user to fire
         gameEnded= 0;
          //hide the intro or game over image
            $('#SZo_4').css({opacity:0});
          //make sure it is out of the way
            $('#SZo_4').css('top', ($(window).height()));

          //show the elements
          for (i = 1; i < 4; i++) {
           //this will get called 3 times
           $('#SZo_'+i).css({opacity:1});
          }//for
        //hide the reload button!
        $('#SZo_2').css({opacity:0});
          //show the zombies
          for (i = 0; i < 7; i++) {
           //reset the Zombie
           SZ_resetZombie(i,0);
          }//for
        //ensure the score board is half opacity
        $('#SZo_3').css({opacity:0.5});

}//end of function
```

Save the file and then close it.

In the start_end_game function, there is a plethora of checks and actions made at one time. As you further this game, this function will become unmanageable, so I suggest that you try to section off the checks to another file so that this function is checking the status of various elements.

One possibility is to set flags for certain conditions. These flags can be set on certain events. This means that when we come to this function, all that we are doing is checking the flag's status.

In the same way, some of the actions should be in a function of their own; for instance, hiding the various elements based on the preceding checks.

Open the SZ_touch.js file and type the following new lines (all new text is in bold) and some modified lines (all in red):

```
//We need a flag to keep track to avoid repetition of
animations before the first has finished
var canIclick= 0;

//this function is called to reload our gun
function reloadGun(e) {
 //Let's check if we can allow this to occur
   if(canIclick== 0 && $("#SZ0_2").css('opacity') == 1){
     //looks like we can so we better set our flag
       canIclick=1;
       $("#SZ0_1").animateSprite("play", "reload");
     //reset the current shots
       current_shots=0;
     //hide the reload button
       $("#SZ0_2").css({opacity:0});
   }
}
```

```
//place a maximum number of shots
var max_shots=5;
//keep track of current number of shots
var current_shots=0;

//this function is called to fire our gun
function fireGun(e) {
 //Let's check if we can allow this to occur
   if(canIclick== 0 && gameEnded==0 && $("#SZo_2").
   css('opacity') != 1){
     //looks like we can so we better set our flag
       canIclick=1;
       $("#SZo_1").animateSprite("play", "fire");
     //increment our shots
       current_shots++;
     //check to see if we have reached the maximum
       if(current_shots>=max_shots){
        //show the reload button
          $("#SZo_2").css({opacity:1});
       }//if
   }
}

//array to keep track of the zombie hits
 var zombieHits_counter = [0,0,0,0,0,0];
//array for each zombies limit
 var zombieHits_limits = [2,1,3,2,1,3];

//this function will keep track of the zombie hits and act
accordingly
function zombieHit(whichOne){

 //increment the counter
```

```
zombieHits_counter[whichOne]++;

//check to see if this zombie has reached its limit
 if(zombieHits_counter[whichOne] >= zombieHits_limits[whichOne]){

    //reset this zombie
    SZ_resetZombie(whichOne+1,1);
  }
}
```

Save the file and then close it.

It is essential to the readability of your code to give meaningful names to variables and functions. This is seen in the preceding code. As your game becomes bigger and more complex, you will cut down on the time needed to understand your previously written code if you can read it like a novel.

Open the SZ_zombie_movement.js file and type the following new lines (all new text is in bold) and some modified lines (all in red):

```
//let's create a zombie
function SZ_createZombie(whichOne){

 //create a new div to hold the zombie SS
   var div = document.createElement('div');
 //and another for the bubble zombie SS
   var div2 = document.createElement('div');

 //we need to hard code the CSS styles we want
   div.setAttribute('style','position: fixed; top:0; left:0;
   opacity:0');
 //and the same for our bubble zombie
   div2.setAttribute('style','position: fixed; top:0; left:0;');

 //we want to position our zombie exactly at the tip of the
 planet
   var top_position= $('#SZ0_0').height() * 0.435;
```

```
//Xpos can be anywhere on our x axis
  var left_position = Math.floor(Math.random() * ($('#SZO_O').
  width())-(ratio*50)) + (ratio*50);

//record this left position
  leftx_zombie[whichOne-1]=left_position;

//let's position our zombie
  div.style.left = left_position+'px'; div.style.top =
  top_position+'px';
//and the same for our bubble zombie
  div2.style.left = left_position+'px'; div2.style.top =
  top_position+'px';

//give it an id
  div.id = 'zombie'+whichOne;
//also for our bubble zombie
  div2.id = 'bubble_zombie'+whichOne;

//finally let's add our zombie to the screen
  document.body.appendChild(div);
//finally add in our bubble zombie to the screen too
  document.body.appendChild(div2);

//put this new zombie through our SS function
 setup_zombie_SS(whichOne);

//put this new zombie through our animate function
 // SZ_animateZombie(whichOne);

//hide the bubble zombies at the start
  $("#bubble_zombie"+whichOne).css('transform','scale('+0+')');

//set the zindex for the zombie
 $("#zombie"+whichOne).css("z-index", whichOne+100);
```

```
//set the zindex for the bubble zombie
 $("#bubble_zombie"+whichOne).css("z-index", whichOne);
//ensure the zindex for the gun is the highest
 $("#SZO_1").css("z-index", 200);
//also ensure the zindex for the intro/game over is the highest
 $("#SZO_4").css("z-index", 201);

//bind the users mouse click to this zombie
$("#zombie"+whichOne).bind('mousedown touchstart', function (e) {
   //make sure the reload button is showing
    if($("#SZO_2").css('opacity') != 1) {
        //first we want to fire the gun
        fireGun(event);
        //acknowledge the hit
if($("#zombie"+whichOne).css('opacity') != 0){
        zombieHit(whichOne-1);
}
    }
  });

//bind the users mouse click to the bubble zombie
 $("#bubble_zombie"+whichOne).bind('mousedown touchstart',
function (e) {
   //make sure the reload button is showing
    if($("#SZO_2").css('opacity') != 1) {
        //first we want to fire the gun
        fireGun(event);

    }
  });

}
```

```
//we need to keep track of the current scale values
 var scalex_zombie = [0,0,0,0,0,0];
//we also need to keep track of the left position
 var leftx_zombie = [0,0,0,0,0,0];

//let's animate our zombie towards us
function SZ_animateZombie(whichOne){

    //assign the speed for each of our zombies
    var timex = [13000,8000,16000,14000,10000,18000];

    //assign a user friendly name for our div
    var $zombiex = $("#zombie"+whichOne);

    //reset the zombies scale value
     $zombiex.css('transform','scale('+0+')');

    //reset the zombies opacity
     $zombiex.css({opacity:1});

    //work out the amount the zombie has to come towards us
    var amty = ($(window).height()*0.7);// -($zombiex.
    height()*2));//topx);

    //each type of zombie will have their own walking style
    var ZS_ease = ['easeInSine','easeOutQuart','easeInOutQuad',
    'easeInSine','easeOutQuart','easeInOutQuad'];

    //finally we are ready to animate
      $zombiex.delay(timex[whichOne-1]/3).animate({
            //first bring our zombie slowly down the screen
            left:  "+="+0.001+ "px",
        },{ easing:ZS_ease[whichOne-1], duration:
        timex[whichOne-1],

          step: function(now, fx){
```

```
//at each step we can manipulate the scale of
our zombie
if (fx.prop == "left") {
//work out the amount to scale
var xx = (fx.pos)*16;
if(gameEnded==1){
 xx=999;
}
//do a check to see if we should end this
animation
        if(xx>15){
            //stop all animation
            $(this).stop();
            //call a function to reset this zombie
            //SZ_resetZombie(whichOne,0);
            //game Over
             $(this).css({opacity:0});
             $(this).stop(true, true);
             $(this).finish();
           if(gameEnded==0 && xx!=999){
           start_end_game(1);
           }
        } else {
            //apply the scale
            $(this).css('transform',
            'scale('+xx+')');
            //record this new scale value
            scalex_zombie[whichOne-1]=xx;

            //check the depth levels
             var i = 0;
             while (i < 6) {
```

```
                            //check to see if the scale is
                            bigger
                            if(scalex_zombie[whichOne-1]>
                            scalex_zombie[i] && ($(this).
                            zIndex() < $("#zombie"+(i+1)).
                            zIndex()) && scalex_zombie[i]!=0){
                              var i_index =
                              $("#zombie"+(i+1)).zIndex();
                              //change the i one first
                              $("#zombie"+(i+1)).css("z-index",
                              $(this).css( "z-index" ));
                              //now change this one
                              $(this).css("z-index", i_index);
                            } //end of if
                                  i++;
                        }//end of while loop
                    }
                }
            }, complete: function () {
                }
            });
}
//need to keep track of the current zindex for zombies
var zindex_current=0;
//a function to completely reset our zombie
function SZ_resetZombie(whichOne, zombieBubble_generate){

    //reset this zombies hit counter
    zombieHits_counter[whichOne-1]=0;

    //assign a user friendly name for our div
    var $zombiex = $("#zombie"+whichOne);
```

```
//we need to stop this zombies animations
 $zombiex.stop();

//we want to position our zombie exactly at the tip of the
planet
 var top_position= $('#SZ0_0').height() * 0.435;

//should we generate a bubble zombie?
 if(zombieBubble_generate==1){
    //assign a user friendly name for our bubble zombie div
     var $bubble_zombiex = $("#bubble_zombie"+whichOne);
    //let's re-position our bubble zombie to our stored
    value
     $bubble_zombiex.css({top: top_position+'px',left:
     $zombiex.css("left"), opacity:1});

    //apply the scale
     $bubble_zombiex.css('transform','scale('+scalex_
     zombie[whichOne-1]+')');
    //call our bubble zombie animation function
     bubbleZombie_flyAway(whichOne);
 }

//Xpos can be anywhere on our x axis
 var left_position = Math.floor(Math.random() *
 ($('#SZ0_0').width())-(ratio*50)) + (ratio*50);

//record this left position
 leftx_zombie[whichOne-1]=left_position;

//let's re-position our zombie
 $zombiex.css({top: top_position+'px', left:
 left_position+'px', opacity:0});

//set the zindex for the zombie
 zindex_current++;
```

```
$("#zombie"+whichOne).css("z-index", zindex_current);

    //finally let's make the zombie come towards the screen
again
        if(zombieBubble_generate==0){
        SZ_animateZombie(whichOne);
        }

}
```

Save the file and then close it.

Go back to the My_Work_Files folder and double-click the default. html file. You should see the intro splash screen straightaway. You should also note that the score and gun images are not there, as we wanted. When we start the game, it should look like as it did before the most recent changes. When a zombie arrives at the end of its path, you should now see the Game Over screen.

Congratulations! You have developed a working game.

Next, let's refine our game to be more presentable for our users.

Did the code not work? We changed a lot of files here, so the advice I give is to meticulously go through every line of code in each of the files and compare it to your own. Even the old grayed out code. Have patience and work through your code.

Here are some problems that I identified:

Make sure that you have the closing tag (shown in red) in the following line:

```
<div id="SZ0_4" onmousedown="start_game();"/>
```

Make sure that you place this line above the main function:

```
    var ratio_use = ratio;
//main function
```

Make sure that you are using ratio_use and not ratio in the following lines:

```
$('#SZ0_4').css('width', 868 * ratio_use);
$('#SZ0_4').css('height', 701 * ratio_use);
```

Make sure that you have commented out (//)the following lines:

```
// SZ_animateZombie(whichOne);
//SZ_resetZombie(whichOne,0);
```

If the code is still not working, then please do not hesitate to message me on Twitter @zarrarchishti.

How does the game know when to show the Intro Splash screen and when to show the Game Over screen?

When called, the following function stops the game and shows either the introduction or the Game Over screen:

```
function start_end_game(whichOne) {
```

One of the tasks of this function is to show either the intro image or the Game Over image, depending on the whichOne passed parameter in. The following lines will show either of those images:

```
$('#SZ0_4').css('background-image', 'url(images/
splash_intro.png)');
$('#SZ0_4').css('background-image', 'url(images/
splash_gameover.png)');
```

CHAPTER 8

Add Some Bling to Our Game

"Simplicity is the ultimate sophistication."

Leonardo da Vinci

I am sure you have noticed that there is no actual score in our Score box. What we need in there is some text that increments every time we send a zombie off into space. To do this, we need to do the following:

1. Add a text field in our HTML.

2. Format this text field so that it changes size and location, depending on the screen size.

3. Start at zero and increment every time a bubble zombie appears.

4. Reset back to zero every time a new game is played.

© Zarrar Chishti 2017
Z. Chishti, *Cross Over to HTML5 Game Development*,
https://doi.org/10.1007/978-1-4842-3291-0_8

What's the Score?

Open the default.html file and type the following new lines (all new text is in bold) and some modified lines (all in red):

```
<html>
 <head>
  <script src="js/jquery.js"></script>
  <script src="js/jquery-ui.js"></script>
  <script src="js/SZ_main.js"></script>
  <script src="js/SZ_setupContent.js"></script>
  <script src="js/SZ_movement.js"></script>
  <script src="js/ss.js"></script>
  <script src="js/SZ_SS.js"></script>
  <script src="js/SZ_touch.js"></script>
  <script src="js/SZ_zombie_movement.js"></script>
  <link href="css/SZ_master.css" rel="stylesheet" />
 </head>
 <body>
  <div id="SZ_maincontent">
   <img id="SZO_0" src="images/SZ_background_image.jpg"
   onmousemove="rotateGun(event)"  onmousedown="fireGun(event)" />
   <div id="SZO_1" ></div>
   <div id="SZO_2" >
    <img  src="images/SZ_reload.png"
    onmousedown="reloadGun(event)" />
   </div>
   <div id="SZO_3" style="background-image: url
   (images/SZ_score.png);">
    <div id="textx">0</div>
   </div>
```

```
<div id="SZ0_4" onmousedown="start_game();"/>
 </div>
</body>
</html>
```

Save this file and then close it.

We have come across background-image a few times in this project. As you can guess, the background-image property sets one or more background images for an element. It is important to remember that a background-image is placed at the top-left corner of an element by default and repeated both vertically and horizontally. So these properties need to be addressed if you want the property to act differently. I always advise setting a background-color property as well. This is in case the image is unavailable or takes too long to load.

Open the SZ_master.css file and type the following new lines (all new text is in bold) and some modified lines (all in red):

```
html {

     height: 100%;

     }
body {

     padding: 0 0 0 0;

     margin: 0;
     user-select: none;
     cursor: crosshair;
     }
img  {

     max-width: 100%;
     height: auto;
     user-drag: none;
     user-select: none;
```

```
        -moz-user-select: none;
        -webkit-user-drag: none;
        -webkit-user-select: none;
        -ms-user-select: none;
    }
#SZ0_0 {
        position: fixed;
        top: 0;
        left: 0;
        min-width: 100%;
        min-height: 100%;
    }
 #SZ0_1 {
        position: fixed;
        bottom: 0;
        right: 0;
        opacity:0;
}
 #SZ0_2 {
        position: fixed;
        top: 0;
        left: 0;
        cursor: pointer;
        opacity:0;
}
 #SZ0_3 {
        position: fixed;
        top: 0;
        right: 0;
        opacity:0;
        background-size:cover;
}
```

```
#SZO_4 {
        position: fixed;
        cursor: pointer;
        background-size:cover;
        opacity:0;
}
 #textx {
        position: relative;
        float: left;
        top: 40%;
        text-align:center;
        font-size: 4vmax;
        font-weight: bolder;
        colour: white;
        font-family: "Arial Black";
}
```

Save this file and then close it.

Nearly done! Now open the SZ_setupContent.js file and type the following new lines (all new text is in bold) and some modified lines:

```
    //we will need a new ratio var
    var ratio_use = ratio;

//main function
  function main_call_setupContent() {
    //need to resize all elements
    //first we set their normal sizes in CSS

    //Gun
    $('#SZO_1').css('width', 150 * ratio);
    $('#SZO_1').css('height', 150 * ratio);
```

```
//Reload Button
 $('#SZO_2').css('width', 200 * ratio);
 $('#SZO_2').css('height', 90 * ratio);

//Score
 $('#SZO_3').css('width', 235 * ratio);
 $('#SZO_3').css('height', 100 * ratio);

//Intro and Game over
if($(window).height()<$(window).width()){
 //work out a ratio based on height
 ratio_use =  $(window).height()/800;
}//end if
//apply this new ratio to our intro/game over
$('#SZO_4').css('width', 868 * ratio_use);
$('#SZO_4').css('height', 701 * ratio_use);
$('#SZO_4').css('left', ($(window).width()/2)
-((868 * ratio_use)/2));
//make sure it is half way
$('#SZO_4').css('top', ($(window).height()/2)
-((701 * ratio_use)/2));

 $('#textx').css('width', '100%');
 $('#textx').css('height', '50%');

//Any sprite sheets?
 //Our Gun
   setup_gun_SS();

//Create all our 6 zombies
 for (i = 1; i < 7; i++) {
 //this will get called 6 times
 SZ_createZombie(i);
 }
```

```
    //call the intro
    start_end_game(0);
}

var gameEnded=0;
//Intro or Game Over of game
  function start_end_game(whichOne) {
          //hide the elements
          for (i = 1; i < 4; i++) {
           //this will get called 3 times
           $('#SZO_'+i).css({opacity:0});
          }//for

          //hide the zombies
          for (i = 1; i < 7; i++) {
          //we need to stop this zombies animations
            $('#zombie_'+i).stop();
            $('#zombie_'+i).css({opacity:0});
            $('#bubble_zombie_'+i).css({opacity:0});
          //set the zindex for the zombie
            $("#zombie"+i).css("z-index", i+100);
          }//for

        if(whichOne==0){
         //START OF GAME
        //change the background image
          $('#SZO_4').css('background-image',
          'url(images/splash_intro.png)');
        } else {
         //GAME OVER
        //show the score
          $('#SZO_3').css({opacity:1});
        //change the background image
```

```
        $('#SZO_4').css('background-image',
        'url(images/splash_gameover.png)');
    }

    //make sure it is half way
    $('#SZO_4').css('top', ($(window).height()/2)
    -((701 * ratio_use)/2));
        //finally show the intro or game over image
        $('#SZO_4').css({opacity:1});

    //stop the user from firing
    gameEnded= 1;

}//end of function

//need to store the current score
var current_score=0;
//we can call this function to update the score
function updateScore(){
 $("#textx").text(current_score);
}

//start the game
  function start_game() {

        //reset the score
        current_score=0;
        updateScore();

    //reset the zindex
    zindex_current=0;

    //reload the gun
    current_shots=0;

    //allow user to fire
    gameEnded= 0;
```

```
    //hide the intro or game over image
    $('#SZO_4').css({opacity:0});
   //make sure it is out of the way
      $('#SZO_4').css('top', ($(window).height()));

   //show the elements
   for (i = 1; i < 4; i++) {
    //this will get called 3 times
    $('#SZO_'+i).css({opacity:1});
   }//for
  //hide the reload button!
  $('#SZO_2').css({opacity:0});

   //show the zombies
   for (i = 0; i < 7; i++) {
    //reset the Zombie
    SZ_resetZombie(i,0);
   }//for
  //ensure the score board is half opacity
  $('#SZO_3').css({opacity:0.5});

}//end of function
```

Save this file and then close it.

As you further develop this game or start a new one, I would suggest you store the z-index values (or even starting values) in another file. This will help in the future when you come to make amendments and need to keep track of what the various elements' z-index values are.

Finally, open the SZ_movement.js file and type the following new lines (all new text is in bold) and some modified lines (all in red):

```
function rotateGun(e) {

//using the e value we can deduce the X co-ordinates
var xPos = e.clientX;

//We need to work out where the mouse cursor is as a percentage
of the width of the screen

//We will work this out by dividing the current X position by the
overall screen width which if you remember we put in newWidth
var currentXPositionPercentage = xPos/newWidth;

//We now want to apply this to the maximum amount of rotation
which is 50 however the starting rotation is -15 not 0
var amountToRotate = -15 + (currentXPositionPercentage * 50);

//Let's rotate the gun!
  $("#SZO_1").css('transform', 'rotate('+amountToRotate+'deg)');

}


//movement for our bubble zombie
function bubbleZombie_flyAway(whichOne){

        //update the score
        current_score++;
        updateScore();

  //assign a user friendly name for our div
    var $zombiex = $("#bubble_zombie"+whichOne);

    //first it should animate upwards with a bounce
      $zombiex.animate({
              //bring our zombie up the screen
              top:   "-="+50*ratio+ "px",
          },{ easing:"easeOutElastic",  duration: 400,
```

```
complete: function () {
    //now the final animation where the bubble
    zombie disappears into space
    $(this).delay(150).animate({
      //slowly turn the alpha down
      opacity:    "-="+1,
    },{ easing:"easeOutQuint",  duration: 1000,

        step: function(now, fx){
            //at each step we can adjust the scale
            to make it look smaller
    if (fx.prop == "opacity" && fx.pos>=0.1) {
        //work out the amount to scale
        var xx = 0.5/(fx.pos);
        //apply the scale
        $(this).css('transform','scale('+xx+')');
    }
    }, complete: function () {
    //finally let's make the zombie come towards
    the screen again
      SZ_animateZombie(whichOne);
    }//end of second complete function
    });//end of second animation
    }//end of first complete function
  }); //end of first animation
}
```

Save this file and then close it.

We are now ready to test! Go back to the My_Work_Files folder and double-click the default.html file. You should now see the score text appear. Every time we send a zombie off into space, you should get a point.

Did this not work? If not, it is most likely the code written in default.html.
Originally, the code was this:

```
<div id="SZo_3" >
 <img src="images/SZ_score.png" />
</div>
```

Now, we are changing it to this:

```
<div id="SZo_3" style="background-image: url(images/
SZ_score.png);">
    <div id="textx">0</div>
    </div>
```

Please make sure that you have coded the lines exactly as shown.

If the code is still not working, then please do not hesitate to message
me on Twitter (@zarrarchishti).

How does updateScore(){ actually update the text on the screen?

As you may have noticed, we initially created a variable called

var current_score=0;

This is then updated using the following line whenever a bubble zombie animation is called:

current_score++;

We know from before that the ++ increments the variable by 1. This alone does not update the text on the screen. Look at the code in our function.

updateScore(){ :
$("#textx").text(current_score);

This replaces the text in our text div with the value in the current score variable. At this point, the screen text value changes.

Sprinkle of Special Effects

You may have noticed there is no visual feedback given to the user when they fire on a zombie. Only when the maximum number of hits has been reached do you see feedback in the form of a bubble zombie. So in this chapter, we add a special effect to the zombie when it has been hit.

Part 1: Get Started

Go to the images folder in the Raw Images folder of the My_Work_Files folder. Locate the file named SZ_effect_ss.png and copy into the Images folder, which should now look like this:

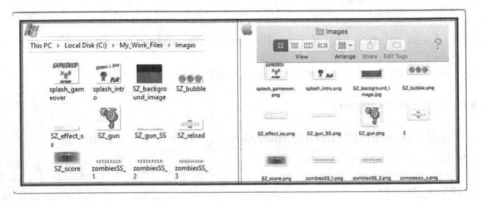

Part 2: Displaying the Effects

To add our special effect to the screen, we need to pinpoint exactly where the user has hit a zombie. Once we have done this, we can then use our sprite sheet library to display our effects.

Open the SZ_zombie_movement.js file and type the following new lines (all new text are in bold) and some modified lines (all in red):

```
//let's create a zombie
function SZ_createZombie(whichOne){

 //create a new div to hold the zombie SS
   var div = document.createElement('div');
 //and another for the bubble zombie SS
   var div2 = document.createElement('div');
 //and another for the special effect SS
   var div3 = document.createElement('div');
```

```
//we need to hard code the CSS styles we want
  div.setAttribute('style','position: fixed; top:0; left:0;
  opacity:0');
//and the same for our bubble zombie
  div2.setAttribute('style','position: fixed; top:0; left:0;');
//and the same for our special effect SS
  div3.setAttribute('style','position: fixed; top:0; left:0;');

//we want to position our zombie exactly at the tip of the planet
  var top_position= $('#SZo_0').height() * 0.435;

//Xpos can be anywhere on our x axis
  var left_position = Math.floor(Math.random() * ($('#SZo_0').
  width())-(ratio*50)) + (ratio*50);

//record this left position
  leftx_zombie[whichOne-1]=left_position;

//let's position our zombie
  div.style.left = left_position+'px'; div.style.top =
  top_position+'px';
//and the same for our bubble zombie
  div2.style.left = left_position+'px'; div2.style.top =
  top_position+'px';
//and the same for our special effect SS
  div3.style.left = left_position+'px'; div3.style.top =
  top_position+'px';

//give it an id
  div.id = 'zombie'+whichOne;
//also for our bubble zombie
  div2.id = 'bubble_zombie'+whichOne;
//also for our special effect SS
  div3.id = 'zombie_effect'+whichOne;
```

```
//finally let's add our zombie to the screen
  document.body.appendChild(div);
//finally add in our bubble zombie to the screen too
  document.body.appendChild(div2);
//finally add in our special effect SS to the screen too
  document.body.appendChild(div3);

//put this new zombie through our SS function
 setup_zombie_SS(whichOne);

//put this new zombie through our animate function
 // SZ_animateZombie(whichOne);

//hide the bubble zombies at the start
  $("#bubble_zombie"+whichOne).css('transform','scale('+0+')');

//ensure no hits are registered on the special effects
$("#zombie_effect"+whichOne).css( 'pointer-events', 'none' );

//set the zindex for the zombie
 $("#zombie"+whichOne).css("z-index", whichOne+100);
//set the zindex for the bubble zombie
 $("#bubble_zombie"+whichOne).css("z-index", whichOne);
//set the zindex for the special effect SS
 $("#zombie_effect"+whichOne).css("z-index", whichOne+150);
//ensure the zindex for the gun is the highest
 $("#SZ0_1").css("z-index", 200);
//also ensure the zindex for the intro/game over is the highest
 $("#SZ0_4").css("z-index", 201);

//bind the users mouse click to this zombie
$("#zombie"+whichOne).bind('mousedown touchstart', function (e) {
  //make sure the reload button is showing
   if($("#SZ0_2").css('opacity') != 1) {
       //first we want to fire the gun
```

```
        fireGun(event);
        //acknowledge the hit
if($("#zombie"+whichOne).css('opacity') != 0){
        var offset = $(this).offset();
        zombieHit(whichOne-1, e.pageX, e.pageY);
}
    }
  });

//bind the users mouse click to the bubble zombie
 $("#bubble_zombie"+whichOne).bind('mousedown touchstart',
function (e) {
   //make sure the reload button is showing
   if($("#SZ0_2").css('opacity') != 1) {
       //first we want to fire the gun
          fireGun(event);

   }
  });

}


//we need to keep track of the current scale values
 var scalex_zombie =  [0,0,0,0,0,0];
//we also need to keep track of the left position
 var leftx_zombie =  [0,0,0,0,0,0];

//let's animate our zombie towards us
function SZ_animateZombie(whichOne){

   //assign the speed for each of our zombies
   var timex =  [13000,8000,16000,14000,10000,18000];

   //assign a user friendly name for our div
   var $zombiex = $("#zombie"+whichOne);
```

```
//reset the zombies scale value
$zombiex.css('transform','scale('+0+')');

//reset the zombies opacity
$zombiex.css({opacity:1});

//work out the amount the zombie has to come towards us
var amty =  ($(window).height()*0.7);
// -($zombiex.height()*2));//topx);

//each type of zombie will have their own walking style
var ZS_ease = ['easeInSine','easeOutQuart','easeInOutQuad',
'easeInSine','easeOutQuart','easeInOutQuad'];

//finally we are ready to animate
  $zombiex.delay(timex[whichOne-1]/3).animate({
          //first bring our zombie slowly down the screen
          left:    "+="+0.001+ "px",
     },{ easing:ZS_ease[whichOne-1],  duration:
     timex[whichOne-1],

         step: function(now, fx){
           //at each step we can manipulate the scale of
           our zombie
           if (fx.prop == "left") {
              //work out the amount to scale
              var xx = (fx.pos)*16;
                 if(gameEnded==1){
                         xx=999;
                 }
           //do a check to see if we should end this animation
               if(xx>15){
                  //stop all animation
                  $(this).stop();
```

```
        //call a function to reset this zombie
        //SZ_resetZombie(whichOne,0);
        //game Over
        $(this).css({opacity:0});
        $(this).stop(true, true);
        $(this).finish();
    if(gameEnded==0 && xx!=999){
        start_end_game(1);
    }
    } else {
        //apply the scale
        $(this).css('transform',
        'scale('+xx+')');
        //record this new scale value
        scalex_zombie[whichOne-1]=xx;
        //check the depth levels
        var i = 0;
        while (i < 6) {
            //check to see if the scale is
            bigger
            if(scalex_zombie[whichOne-1]
            >scalex_zombie[i] &&
            ($(this).zIndex() <
            $("#zombie"+(i+1)).zIndex())
            && scalex_zombie[i]!=0){
            var i_index =
            $("#zombie"+(i+1)).zIndex();
            //change the i one first
            $("#zombie"+(i+1)).css("z-index",
            $(this).css( "z-index" ));
            //now change this one
```

```
                                    $(this).css("z-index",
                                        i_index);
                                } //end of if
                            i++;
                        }//end of while loop
                    }
                }
            }, complete: function () {
                }
        });
}
```

```
//need to keep track of the current zindex for zombies
var zindex_current=0;
```

```
//a function to completely reset our zombie
function SZ_resetZombie(whichOne, zombieBubble_generate){
```

```
    //reset this zombies hit counter
     zombieHits_counter[whichOne-1]=0;
```

```
    //assign a user friendly name for our div
     var $zombiex = $("#zombie"+whichOne);
```

```
    //we need to stop this zombies animations
     $zombiex.stop();
```

```
    //we want to position our zombie exactly at the tip of the
    planet
     var top_position= $('#SZ0_0').height() * 0.435;
```

```
    //should we generate a bubble zombie?
     if(zombieBubble_generate==1){
        //assign a user friendly name for our bubble zombie div
         var $bubble_zombiex = $("#bubble_zombie"+whichOne);
```

```
        //let's re-position our bubble zombie to our stored value
        $bubble_zombiex.css({top: top_position+'px',left:
        $zombiex.css("left"), opacity:1});

        //apply the scale
        $bubble_zombiex.css('transform','scale('+scalex_
        zombie[whichOne-1]+')');
        //call our bubble zombie animation function
        bubbleZombie_flyAway(whichOne);
    }
    //Xpos can be anywhere on our x axis
    var left_position = Math.floor(Math.random() *
    ($('#SZO_0').width())-(ratio*50)) + (ratio*50);

    //record this left position
    leftx_zombie[whichOne-1]=left_position;

    //let's re-position our zombie
    $zombiex.css({top: top_position+'px', left:
    left_position+'px', opacity:0});
//set the zindex for the zombie
zindex_current++;
  $("#zombie"+whichOne).css("z-index", zindex_current);

    //finally let's make the zombie come towards the screen again
      if(zombieBubble_generate==0){
      SZ_animateZombie(whichOne);
      }
}
```

Save the file and then close it.

We referenced e.pageX and e.pageY properties in the preceding code. They return the position of the mouse pointer relative to the left edge of the document. These properties take into account any horizontal or vertical scrolling of the page. In case you are referencing some older code in the future, this property was originally defined as a long integer; however, the CSSOM View Module redefined it as a double float.

Open the SZ_touch.js file and type the following new lines (all new text is in bold) and some modified lines (all in red):

```
  //We need a flag to keep track to avoid repetition of
animations before the first has finished
var canIclick= 0;

//this function is called to reload our gun
function reloadGun(e) {
 //Let's check if we can allow this to occur
   if(canIclick== 0 && $("#SZO_2").css('opacity') == 1){
    //looks like we can so we better set our flag
      canIclick=1;
      $("#SZO_1").animateSprite("play", "reload");
    //reset the current shots
      current_shots=0;
    //hide the reload button
      $("#SZO_2").css({opacity:0});
    }

}

//place a maximum number of shots
var max_shots=5;
//keep track of current number of shots
var current_shots=0;

//this function is called to fire our gun
function fireGun(e) {
```

```
//Let's check if we can allow this to occur
  if(canIclick== 0 && gameEnded==0 && $("#SZ0_2").css
  ('opacity') != 1){
    //looks like we can so we better set our flag
      canIclick=1;
      $("#SZ0_1").animateSprite("play", "fire");
    //increment our shots
      current_shots++;
    //check to see if we have reached the maximum
      if(current_shots>=max_shots){
       //show the reload button
         $("#SZ0_2").css({opacity:1});
       }//if
  }
}

//array to keep track of the zombie hits
 var zombieHits_counter = [0,0,0,0,0,0];
//array for each zombies limit
 var zombieHits_limits = [2,1,3,2,1,3];
```

//this function will keep track of the zombie hits and act accordingly

```
function zombieHit(whichOne, xx, yy){

 //increment the counter
  zombieHits_counter[whichOne]++;

 //check to see if this zombie has reached its limit
  if(zombieHits_counter[whichOne] >= zombieHits_
  limits[whichOne]){

   //reset this zombie
    SZ_resetZombie(whichOne+1,1);
  }
```

```
        //let's add in our special effect
        var whichOne2=whichOne+1;
    var $effect_zombiex = $("#zombie_effect"+whichOne2);
        //let's re-position our bubble zombie to our stored value
        $effect_zombiex.css({top: yy+'px',left: xx+'px',
        opacity:1});
        $effect_zombiex.animateSprite("play", "z1");
        //apply the scale

        $effect_zombiex.css('transform',
        'scale('+scalex_zombie[whichOne]+')');
}
```

Save the file and then close it.

In the preceding code, we dynamically position our special effect to appear exactly on the zombie's div. In some cases, depending on the size of your special effect sprite, you may need to take other factors into consideration. For example, some effects may need to be positioned on an element other than a zombie. You may want a special effect to show that when the user shoots the ground, chunks of the ground are blown up. This is not very hard; we would replace the ground's div with the zombie div.

Where it becomes a slight challenge is when we offset the shooting area so it could include the zombie's foot and the ground area—giving an overall realistic scene where the ground effect and the zombie-hit effect are triggered. As I suggested, we would need to accommodate for both events.

Open the SZ_SS.js file and type the following new lines (all new text is in bold):

```
//We need a one stop function that will allow us to process
sprite sheets
function setup_SpriteSheet(div_name, image_name, no_of_frames,
widthx, heightx) {

 //need the ratio of the container's width/height
  var imageOrgRatio =  $(div_name).height() /
  $(div_name).width() ;

 //need to ensure no trailing decimals
  var ratio2 = Math.round(ratio * 10) / 10;

 //check that the width is completely divisible by the no of
 frames
  var newDivisible = Math.round((widthx * ratio2) /
  no_of_frames);

 //the new width will be the number of frames multiplied by our
 new divisible
  var newWidthx = newDivisible * no_of_frames;

 //also the new height will be our ratio times the height of
 the div containing our image
  var newHeightx = heightx * ratio2;

 //apply our new width to our CSS
  $(div_name).css('width', (newWidthx));

 //apply our new height to our CSS
  $(div_name).css('height', newHeightx);
//
 //take the image name and apply as a background image to our div
  $(div_name).css('background-image', 'url(' + image_name + ')');

 //finally we need to apply a background size remembering we
 need to multiply width by the no of frames
```

```
        $(div_name).css('background-size', newWidthx * no_of_frames
        + 'px ' + newHeightx + 'px');
}

//setup the Gun
function setup_gun_SS(){
 //first let's apply our gun to our SS function
    setup_SpriteSheet("#SZO_1","Images/SZ_gun_SS.png",28,150,150);
 //need to access a special function in our js/ss.js file
    $("#SZO_1").animateSprite({
        fps: 10,
        animations: {
            static: [0],
            reload: [1,2,3,4,5,6,7,8,9,10,11,12,13,14,15,16,17,
            18,19,20,21,22,23],
            fire: [24,25,26,27,28],
        },
        duration: 50,
        loop: false,
        complete: function () {
            // use complete only when you set animations with
            'loop: false'
            //alert("animation End");
            //we need to reset our universal flag
              canIclick=0;
        }
    });
}

//setup a newly created zombie
function setup_zombie_SS(whichOne){

 //let's identify what type of zombie we should create
    var type_zombie = [1,2,3,1,2,3];
```

```
//let's setup a speed for each type of zombie
  var speed_zombie = [100,50,150];

//first let's setup our zombie SS

  setup_SpriteSheet("#zombie"+whichOne,"Images/zombiesSS_"
  +type_zombie[whichOne-1]+".png",9,20,20);
//need to access a special function in our js/ss.js file
    $("#zombie"+whichOne).animateSprite({
        fps: 10,
        animations: {
            static: [0,1,2,3,4,5,6,7],
        },
        duration: speed_zombie[type_zombie[whichOne-1]-1],
        loop: true,
        complete: function () {
            // use complete only when you set animations with
            'loop: false'
            //alert("animation End");
        }
    });

//now let's setup our bubble zombie SS

  setup_SpriteSheet("#bubble_zombie"+whichOne,
  "Images/SZ_bubble.png",3,20,20);
//need to access a special function in our js/ss.js file
    $("#bubble_zombie"+whichOne).animateSprite({
        fps: 10,
        animations: {
            z1: [type_zombie[whichOne-1]-1],
        },
        duration: 1,
        loop: false,
```

```
        complete: function () {
            // use complete only when you set animations with
            'loop: false'
            //alert("animation End");
        }
    });
//not to forget our special effects SS
setup_SpriteSheet("#zombie_effect"+whichOne,"Images/SZ_effect_
ss.png",4,13,15);
//need to access a special function in our js/ss.js file
    $("#zombie_effect"+whichOne).animateSprite({
        fps: 10,
        animations: {
            z1: [0,1,2,3],
        },
        duration: 20,
        loop: false,
        complete: function () {
            // use complete only when you set animations with
            'loop: false'
            //alert("animation End");
            $("#zombie_effect"+whichOne).css({opacity:0});
        }
    });
}
```

Save the file and then close it.

We are now ready to test! Go back to the My_Work_Files folder and double-click the default.html file. Now when you fire on the zombies, you should see our special effect appear exactly where you click. I am sure you will agree that this adds a nice depth to the game playing experience for our players!

How did we position the special effects exactly where we click?

To position the special effects, we first need to ensure that we pass through the x and y coordinates when there is a mouse click on a zombie. We do this in SZ_zombie_movement.js.

```
var offset = $(this).offset();
zombieHit(whichOne-1, e.pageX, e.pageY);
```

The offset() method returns the coordinates for us. We can then pass them through to our zombieHit function. This means that we have to modify the zombieHit function in SZ_touch.js.

```
function zombieHit(whichOne, xx, yy){
```

We have added two variables that can be passed in for us to use now.

```
$effect_zombiex.css({top: yy+'px',left: xx+'px', opacity:1});
```

So when we come to position our special effect, we can use our two new variables for the x and y positions.

Turn up the Sound Effects

We noticed that by adding special effects, we could enhance the user's playing experience. Similarly, we can go one step further and provide audio feedback for the various actions that the player performs.

Part 1: Getting Started

Go to the images folder in the Raw Images folder of the My_Work_Files folder. Locate the folder named sounds and copy this into the My_Work_Files folder.

Your My_Work_Files folder should now look like this:

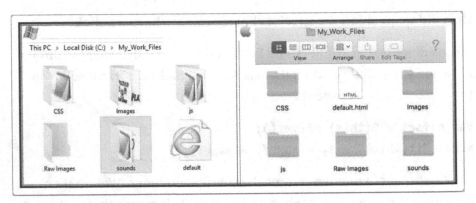

Part 2: Adding Sound Effects

We are going to add two sound effects to our game. The first will be when the player fires their gun. The second will be when the player reloads. Getting the game to play the sounds is not that hard, but controlling when the sounds play is where it can get tricky.

Open the default.html file and type the following new lines (all new text is in bold):

```
<html>
 <head>
  <script src="js/jquery.js"></script>
  <script src="js/jquery-ui.js"></script>
  <script src="sounds/jquery.playSound.js"></script>
  <script src="js/SZ_main.js"></script>
  <script src="js/SZ_setupContent.js"></script>
```

```html
    <script src="js/SZ_movement.js"></script>
    <script src="js/ss.js"></script>
    <script src="js/SZ_SS.js"></script>
    <script src="js/SZ_touch.js"></script>
    <script src="js/SZ_zombie_movement.js"></script>
    <link href="css/SZ_master.css" rel="stylesheet" />
  </head>
  <body>
   <div id="SZ_maincontent">
    <img id="SZO_0" src="images/SZ_background_image.jpg"
    onmousemove="rotateGun(event)"  onmousedown="fireGun(event)" />
    <div id="SZO_1" ></div>
    <div id="SZO_2" >
     <img  src="images/SZ_reload.png"
     onmousedown="reloadGun(event)" />
    </div>
    <div id="SZO_3" style="background-image:
    url(images/SZ_score.png);">
     <div id="textx">999</div>
    </div>
    <div id="SZO_4" onmousedown="start_game();"/>
   </div>
  </body>
</html>
```

Save the file and then close it.

You can certainly source your own sound library or even write your own! The type of library you choose, however, depends on your game's requirements. For instance, in our game we require short sound blasts but not long music files.

At the very basic level, you can use the <audio> tag and then call the play() method.

Open the SZ_touch.js file and type the following new lines (all new text is in bold):

```
//We need a flag to keep track to avoid repetition of animations
before the first has finished
var canIclick= 0;

//this function is called to reload our gun
function reloadGun(e) {
 //Let's check if we can allow this to occur
   if(canIclick== 0 && $("#SZ0_2").css('opacity') == 1){
     //looks like we can so we better set our flag
       canIclick=1;
       $("#SZ0_1").animateSprite("play", "reload");
     //reset the current shots
       current_shots=0;
     //hide the reload button
       $("#SZ0_2").css({opacity:0});
     //play the reload sound
       $.playSound('sounds/reload');
     }
}

//place a maximum number of shots
var max_shots=5;
//keep track of current number of shots
var current_shots=0;

//this function is called to fire our gun
function fireGun(e) {
 //Let's check if we can allow this to occur
   if(canIclick== 0 && gameEnded==0 && $("#SZ0_2").css
   ('opacity') != 1){
```

```
     //looks like we can so we better set our flag
       canIclick=1;
       $("#SZO_1").animateSprite("play", "fire");
       //increment our shots
       current_shots++;
     //play the fire sound
       $.playSound('sounds/fire');
       //check to see if we have reached the maximum
       if(current_shots>=max_shots){
         //show the reload button
           $("#SZO_2").css({opacity:1});
       }//if
   }
}

//array to keep track of the zombie hits
 var zombieHits_counter = [0,0,0,0,0,0];
//array for each zombies limit
 var zombieHits_limits = [2,1,3,2,1,3];

//this function will keep track of the zombie hits and act
accordingly
function zombieHit(whichOne, xx, yy){

 //increment the counter
  zombieHits_counter[whichOne]++;

 //check to see if this zombie has reached its limit
  if(zombieHits_counter[whichOne] >= zombieHits_limits[whichOne]){

    //reset this zombie
    SZ_resetZombie(whichOne+1,1);
  }
```

```
    //let's add in our special effect
    var whichOne2=whichOne+1;
    var $effect_zombiex = $("#zombie_effect"+whichOne2);
    //let's re-position our bubble zombie to our stored value
     $effect_zombiex.css({top: yy+'px',left: xx+'px',
     opacity:1});

  $effect_zombiex.animateSprite("play", "z1");
   //apply the scale

    $effect_zombiex.css('transform',
    'scale('+scalex_zombie[whichOne]+')');
}
```

Save the file and then close it.

We are now ready to test! Go back to the My_Work_Files folder and double-click the default.html file. Now when you fire your gun, you should hear a sound. Also, when you press the Reload button, you should hear the reload sound. Again, I am sure you will agree that this adds a much needed dimension to our game.

Did the sound not work? First, make sure that you have written the following line as it is shown in your default.html.

<script src="sounds/jquery.playSound.js"></script>

Also, make sure that you have the sounds folder copied, as shown in Part 1.

If it is still not working, make sure that the following lines are copied as shown here; pay attention to the lowercase letters.

```
$.playSound('sounds/reload');
$.playSound('sounds/fire');
```

If is still not working, then please do not hesitate to message me on Twitter (@zarrarchishti).

Embedding the Game

You have noticed that the game spans your entire browser window. Although a few games do play in this manner, most games are embedded in a smaller window. We are going to place all of our code to fit inside a window by using a few tweaks to our files.

Part 1: Getting Started

Go to the images folder in the Raw Images folder of the My_Work_Files folder. Locate the folder named html_web and copy this to the My_Work_Files folder, which should now look like this:

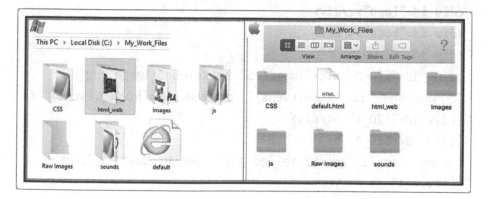

Part 2: Modify the default.html File

To embed the game, we first need to modify the default.html file.
Opening the default.html file and type the following new lines (all new
text is in bold):

```
<html>
 <head>
  <script src="js/jquery.js"></script>
  <script src="js/jquery-ui.js"></script>
  <script src="sounds/jquery.playSound.js"></script>
  <script src="js/SZ_main.js"></script>
  <script src="js/SZ_setupContent.js"></script>
  <script src="js/SZ_movement.js"></script>
  <script src="js/ss.js"></script>
  <script src="js/SZ_SS.js"></script>
  <script src="js/SZ_touch.js"></script>
  <script src="js/SZ_zombie_movement.js"></script>
  <link href="css/SZ_master.css" rel="stylesheet" />
 </head>
 <body>
  <div id="logo"></div>
  <div id="box1"></div>
  <div id="SZ_maincontent">
   <img id="SZO_0" src="images/SZ_background_image.jpg"
   onmousemove="rotateGun(event)"  onmousedown="fireGun(event)" />
   <div id="SZO_1" ></div>
   <div id="SZO_2" >
    <img  src="images/SZ_reload.png"  onmousedown="reloadGun
    (event)" />
   </div>
   <div id="SZO_3" style="background-image:
   url(images/SZ_score.png);">
```

```
    <div id="textx">999</div>
  </div>
  <div id="SZo_4" onmousedown="start_game();"/>
  </div>
 </body>
</html>
```

Save the file and then close it.

Now open the SZ_master.css file and type the following new lines (all new text is in bold) and some modified lines (all in red):

```
html {
      height: 100%;
      background: url(../html_web/webBG.jpg);
      background-size:cover;
}

body {

      padding: 0 0 0 0;

      margin: 0;
      user-select: none;
      cursor: crosshair;
    }
img  {
      max-width: 100%;
      height: 100%;
      user-drag: none;
      user-select: none;
      -moz-user-select: none;
      -webkit-user-drag: none;
      -webkit-user-select: none;
      -ms-user-select: none;
```

```
        }
#logo {
        position: absolute;
        z-index:9999;
        background: url(../html_web/logo.png);
        background-size:cover;
        pointer-events:none;
}
#box1 {
        position: absolute;
        z-index:9998;
        background: url(../html_web/box.png);
        background-size:cover;
        pointer-events:none;
}
#SZ_maincontent {
        position: relative;
        overflow: hidden;
}
#SZ0_0 {
        position: absolute;
        top: 0;
        left: 0;
        min-width: 100%;
        min-height: 100%;
    }
 #SZ0_1 {
        position: absolute;
        bottom: 0;
        right: 0;
        opacity:0;
}
```

```css
#SZO_2 {
        position: absolute;
        top: 0;
        left: 0;
        cursor: pointer;
        opacity:0;
}
#SZO_3 {
        position: absolute;
        top: 0;
        right: 0;
        opacity:0;
        background-size:cover;
}
#SZO_4 {
        position: absolute;
        cursor: pointer;
        background-size:cover;
        opacity:0;
}
#textx {
        position: relative;
        float: left;
        top: 40%;
        text-align:center;
        font-size: 4vmax;
        font-weight: bolder;
        colour: white;
        font-family: "Arial Black";
}
```

Save this file and then close it.

You are nearly done. Open the SZ_setupContent.js file and type the following new lines (all new text is in bold) and some modified lines (all in red):

```
    //we will need a new ratio var
  var ratio_use = ratio;

//main function
  function main_call_setupContent() {
    //need to resize all elements
    //first we set their normal sizes in CSS

//Main Div
    $('#SZ_maincontent').css('width', 600 * ratio);
    $('#SZ_maincontent').css('height', 400 * ratio);
    //make sure it is half way
    $('#SZ_maincontent').css('left',
    ($(window).width()/2)-((600 * ratio)/2));
    $('#SZ_maincontent').css('top',
    ($(window).height()/2)-((400 * ratio)/2));

//box1
    $('#box1').css('width', 631 * ratio);
    $('#box1').css('height', 457 * ratio);
    //make sure it is half way
    $('#box1').css('left', ($(window).width()/2)-
    ((637 * ratio)/2));
    $('#box1').css('top', ($(window).height()/2)-
    ((457 * ratio)/2));

//logo
    $('#logo').css('width', 400 * ratio);
    $('#logo').css('height', 146 * ratio);
```

```
//make sure it is half way
$('#logo').css('left', 0);
$('#logo').css('top', 0);

//Gun
$('#SZ0_1').css('width', 150 * ratio);
$('#SZ0_1').css('height', 150 * ratio);

//Reload Button
$('#SZ0_2').css('width', 200 * ratio);
$('#SZ0_2').css('height', 90 * ratio);

//Score
$('#SZ0_3').css('width', 235 * ratio);
$('#SZ0_3').css('height', 100 * ratio);

//Intro and Game over
if($(window).height()<$(window).width()){
  //work out a ratio based on height
  ratio_use =  $(window).height()/800;
}//end if
//apply this new ratio to our intro/game over
$('#SZ0_4').css('width', 458 * ratio);
$('#SZ0_4').css('height', 370 * ratio);
$('#SZ0_4').css('left', 71 * ratio);
// $('#SZ0_4').css('left', ($(window).width()/2)-
((600 * ratio_use)/2));
//make sure it is half way
//$('#SZ0_4').css('top', ($(window).height()/2)-
((400 * ratio_use)/2));

$('#textx').css('width', '100%');
$('#textx').css('height', '50%');

//Any sprite sheets?
```

```
    //Our Gun
        setup_gun_SS();

  //Create all our 6 zombies
   for (i = 1; i < 7; i++) {
    //this will get called 6 times
    SZ_createZombie(i);
    }

  //call the intro
    start_end_game(0);
}

var gameEnded=0;
//Intro or Game Over of game
  function start_end_game(whichOne) {
            //hide the elements
            for (i = 1; i < 4; i++) {
             //this will get called 3 times
             $('#SZO_'+i).css({opacity:0});
            }//for

            //hide the zombies
            for (i = 1; i < 7; i++) {
            //we need to stop this zombies animations
             $('#zombie_'+i).stop();
             $('#zombie_'+i).css({opacity:0});
             $('#bubble_zombie_'+i).css({opacity:0});
            //set the zindex for the zombie
             $("#zombie"+i).css("z-index", i+100);
            }//for

         if(whichOne==0){
          //START OF GAME
```

```
    //change the background image
     $('#SZ0_4').css('background-image',
     'url(images/splash_intro.png)');
    } else {
     //GAME OVER
    //show the score
     $('#SZ0_3').css({opacity:1});
    //change the background image
     $('#SZ0_4').css('background-image',
     'url(images/splash_gameover.png)');
    }

    //make sure it is half way
      $('#SZ0_4').css('top', 0);
      //finally show the intro or game over image
      $('#SZ0_4').css({opacity:1});

    //stop the user from firing
     gameEnded= 1;

}//end of function

//need to store the current score
var current_score=0;

//we can call this function to update the score
function updateScore(){
 $("#textx").text(current_score);
}

//start the game
  function start_game() {

        //reset the score
         current_score=0;
         updateScore();
```

```
      //reset the zindex
      zindex_current=0;

      //reload the gun
      current_shots=0;

      //allow user to fire
      gameEnded= 0;

        //hide the intro or game over image
        $('#SZO_4').css({opacity:0});
      //make sure it is out of the way
          $('#SZO_4').css('top', ($(window).height()));

       //show the elements
       for (i = 1; i < 4; i++) {
        //this will get called 3 times
        $('#SZO_'+i).css({opacity:1});
       }//for
      //hide the reload button!
      $('#SZO_2').css({opacity:0});

        //show the zombies
        for (i = 0; i < 7; i++) {
         //reset the Zombie
         SZ_resetZombie(i,0);
        }//for
      //ensure the score board is half opacity
      $('#SZO_3').css({opacity:0.5});

}//end of function
```

Save this file and then close it.

Finally, open the SZ_zombie_movement.js file and type the following new lines (all new text is in bold) and some modified lines (all in red):

```
//let's create a zombie
function SZ_createZombie(whichOne){

//create a new div to hold the zombie SS
  var div = document.createElement('div');
//and another for the bubble zombie SS
  var div2 = document.createElement('div');
//and another for the special effect SS
  var div3 = document.createElement('div');

//we need to hard code the CSS styles we want
  div.setAttribute('style','position: fixed; top:0; left:0;
  opacity:0; position: absolute; display: inherit;');
//and the same for our bubble zombie
  div2.setAttribute('style','position: fixed; top:0; left:0;
  position: absolute;');
//and the same for our special effect SS
  div3.setAttribute('style','position: fixed; top:0; left:0;
  position: absolute;');

//we want to position our zombie exactly at the tip of the
planet
  var top_position= $('#SZ0_0').height() * 0.435;

//Xpos can be anywhere on our x axis
  var left_position = Math.floor(Math.random() * ($('#SZ0_0').
  width())-(ratio*50)) + (ratio*50);

//record this left position
  leftx_zombie[whichOne-1]=left_position;
```

```
//let's position our zombie
  div.style.left = left_position+'px'; div.style.top =
  top_position+'px';
//and the same for our bubble zombie
  div2.style.left = left_position+'px'; div2.style.top =
  top_position+'px';
//and the same for our special effect SS
  div3.style.left = left_position+'px'; div3.style.top =
  top_position+'px';

//give it an id
  div.id = 'zombie'+whichOne;
//also for our bubble zombie
  div2.id = 'bubble_zombie'+whichOne;
//also for our special effect SS
  div3.id = 'zombie_effect'+whichOne;

//finally let's add our zombie to the screen
  //document.body.appendChild(div);
    $('#SZ_maincontent').append(div);
//finally add in our bubble zombie to the screen too
  //document.body.appendChild(div2);
    $('#SZ_maincontent').append(div2);
//finally add in our special effect SS to the screen too
  document.body.appendChild(div3);

//put this new zombie through our SS function
 setup_zombie_SS(whichOne);

//put this new zombie through our animate function
 // SZ_animateZombie(whichOne);

//hide the bubble zombies at the start
  $("#bubble_zombie"+whichOne).css('transform','scale('+0+')');
```

```
//ensure no hits are registered on the special effects
$("#zombie_effect"+whichOne).css( 'pointer-events', 'none' );

  //set the zindex for the zombie
  $("#zombie"+whichOne).css("z-index", whichOne+100);
  //set the zindex for the bubble zombie
  $("#bubble_zombie"+whichOne).css("z-index", whichOne);
  //set the zindex for the special effect SS
  $("#zombie_effect"+whichOne).css("z-index", whichOne+150);
  //ensure the zindex for the gun is the highest
  $("#SZO_1").css("z-index", 200);
  //also ensure the zindex for the intro/game over is the highest
  $("#SZO_4").css("z-index", 201);

  //bind the users mouse click to this zombie
  $("#zombie"+whichOne).bind('mousedown touchstart', function (e) {
    //make sure the reload button is showing
    if($("#SZO_2").css('opacity') != 1) {
        //first we want to fire the gun
        fireGun(event);
        //acknowledge the hit
if($("#zombie"+whichOne).css('opacity') != 0){
        var offset = $(this).offset();
        zombieHit(whichOne-1, e.pageX, e.pageY);
}
    }
  });

//bind the users mouse click to the bubble zombie
 $("#bubble_zombie"+whichOne).bind('mousedown touchstart',
function (e) {
   //make sure the reload button is showing
   if($("#SZO_2").css('opacity') != 1) {
```

```
        //first we want to fire the gun
        fireGun(event);

    }
  });
}
```

```
//we need to keep track of the current scale values
 var scalex_zombie =  [0,0,0,0,0,0];
//we also need to keep track of the left position
 var leftx_zombie =  [0,0,0,0,0,0];
```

```
//let's animate our zombie towards us
function SZ_animateZombie(whichOne){

    //assign the speed for each of our zombies
    var timex =  [13000,8000,16000,14000,10000,18000];

    //assign a user friendly name for our div
    var $zombiex = $("#zombie"+whichOne);

    //reset the zombies scale value
     $zombiex.css('transform','scale('+0+')');

    //reset the zombies opacity
     $zombiex.css({opacity:1});

    //work out the amount the zombie has to come towards us
     var amty =  ($(window).height()*0.7);// -
    ($zombiex.height()*2));//topx);

    //each type of zombie will have their own walking style
     var ZS_ease = ['easeInSine','easeOutQuart','easeInOutQuad',
     'easeInSine','easeOutQuart','easeInOutQuad'];

    //finally we are ready to animate
       $zombiex.delay(timex[whichOne-1]/3).animate({
```

```
        //first bring our zombie slowly down the screen
        left:    "+="+0.001+ "px",
},{ easing:ZS_ease[whichOne-1],
duration: timex[whichOne-1],

    step: function(now, fx){
    //at each step we can manipulate the scale of
    our zombie
    if (fx.prop == "left") {
        //work out the amount to scale
        var xx = (fx.pos)*16;
            if(gameEnded==1){
                    xx=999;
            }
    //do a check to see if we should end this animation
            if(xx>15){
                //stop all animation
                $(this).stop();
                //call a function to reset this zombie
                //SZ_resetZombie(whichOne,0);
                //game Over
                 $(this).css({opacity:0});
                 $(this).stop(true, true);
                 $(this).finish();
               if(gameEnded==0 && xx!=999){
                 start_end_game(1);
                 }
            } else {
                //apply the scale
                $(this).css('transform',
                'scale('+xx+')');
                //record this new scale value
                scalex_zombie[whichOne-1]=xx;
```

```
                        //check the depth levels
                        var i = 0;
                        while (i < 6) {
                            //check to see if the scale is
                            bigger
                                if(scalex_zombie[whichOne-1]>
                                scalex_zombie[i] &&
                                ($(this).zIndex() <
                                $("#zombie"+(i+1)).zIndex())
                                && scalex_zombie[i]!=0){
                                var i_index =
                                $("#zombie"+(i+1)).zIndex();
                                //change the i one first
                                $("#zombie"+(i+1)).css
                                ("z-index", $(this).css
                                ( "z-index" ));
                                //now change this one
                                $(this).css("z-index", i_index);
                                } //end of if
                            i++;
                        }//end of while loop
                    }
                }
            }, complete: function () {
                }
            });
}

//need to keep track of the current zindex for zombies
var zindex_current=0;

//a function to completely reset our zombie
function SZ_resetZombie(whichOne, zombieBubble_generate){
```

```
//reset this zombies hit counter
 zombieHits_counter[whichOne-1]=0;

//assign a user friendly name for our div
 var $zombiex = $("#zombie"+whichOne);

//we need to stop this zombies animations
 $zombiex.stop();

//we want to position our zombie exactly at the tip of the
planet
 var top_position= $('#SZO_0').height() * 0.435;

//should we generate a bubble zombie?
 if(zombieBubble_generate==1){
    //assign a user friendly name for our bubble zombie div
     var $bubble_zombiex = $("#bubble_zombie"+whichOne);
    //let's re-position our bubble zombie to our stored
    value
     $bubble_zombiex.css({top: top_position+'px',
     left: $zombiex.css("left"), opacity:1});

    //apply the scale
     $bubble_zombiex.css('transform',
     'scale('+scalex_zombie[whichOne-1]+')');
    //call our bubble zombie animation function
     bubbleZombie_flyAway(whichOne);
 }
//Xpos can be anywhere on our x axis
 var left_position = Math.floor(Math.random() *
 ($('#SZO_0').width())-(ratio*50)) + (ratio*50);

//record this left position
 leftx_zombie[whichOne-1]=left_position;
```

```
    //let's re-position our zombie
    $zombiex.css({top: top_position+'px', left:
    left_position+'px', opacity:0});

//set the zindex for the zombie
zindex_current++;
 $("#zombie"+whichOne).css("z-index", zindex_current);

    //finally let's make the zombie come towards the screen again
      if(zombieBubble_generate==0){
      SZ_animateZombie(whichOne);
      }

}
```

Save this file and then close it.

We are now ready to test! Go back to the My_Work_Files folder and double-click the default.html file. You should see the following screen:

You will agree that, with just a few tweaks of code, we have created a huge improvement in the overall design of our game.

Did it not work? A lot of the code written here are changes to code that was already written. It is important to go through the bolded code line by line and ensure that it looks exactly as shown.

Pay careful attention to the changes in SZ_master.css, especially where we have added the same line to several places.

Finally, take care with changes like this:

```
// $('#SZ0_4').css('left', ($(window).width()/2)-
((600 * ratio_use)/2));
```

Please make sure that you have coded the lines exactly as shown.

If it is still not working, then please do not hesitate to message me on Twitter (@zarrarchishti).

How did the game get smaller?

The game itself is exactly the same; all we did was reduce the amount of space the game takes on the screen:

```
$('#SZ_maincontent').css('width', 600 * ratio);
$('#SZ_maincontent').css('height', 400 * ratio);
```

How did we put the extra graphics on the screen?

Let's take each one separately. The box that surrounds our game is created in the following line:

```
<div id="box1"></div>
```

The logo at the top left was created using

```
<div id="logo"></div>
```

Finally, we put the background image using

```
background: url(../html_web/webBG.jpg); background-size:cover;
```

Game Over. Restart?

This concludes our development. I hope that you enjoyed coding this game as much as I have. I also hope that you have developed a passion for game development and that you go on to create some truly awesome games.

Please contact me if you have any problems or wish to discuss your ideas for other games.

244

Wondering where to go from here? I have put together a few ideas on ways to further develop the game, which you should be able to do on your own now.

- If you are a database developer, you may want to record the scores to a local or server database. To go one step further, you may want to create a screen to capture the user's information, such as their email address.

- Have a small spider-like animation created into sprite sheets. Include this in the gameplay at random intervals. When the user shoots it, give them double points.

- We have explored some options within each chapter (e.g., installing a "head shot" feature). It might be worth going back to revisit these suggestions and try to rewrite the code yourself.

- Place a Pause button. As the name suggests, when clicked, all gameplay should pause. I usually display a fullscreen image, which resumes the game play when clicked.

- Create levels! You will need some way to stop the gameplay and reset all the gameplay parameters. Also, you will want to give some thought as to why each level is different. I would introduce Professor Z in level 1, and then Belladonna in level 2, and, finally, Brad in level 3. In the final stage, I would have all three zombies come out in a random order.

- Finally, get creative! Use this engine for something completely different. For instance, I used the same engine to create a circus-themed game. In this game, the gun was replaced with a rifle and the zombies were replaced with three different types of targets to shoot (e.g., a duck). The targets would move from left to right and move in three different depths. Although I had to change the graphics and tweak the code slightly, the engine for the game remained the same.

Let me know what other games you managed to create using this engine. Join me on Twitter (@zarrarchishti) and let's discuss!

Index

A

Absolute, 35
alert(), 41, 127, 128
animateSprite function, 66
Animation, 13, 23, 51, 66, 68, 70, 73,
     76, 80, 81, 85, 95, 136, 148,
     203, 245
appendChild(), 124
Aptana, 6
Arrays, 47, 93, 94, 97, 113

B

Background-colour, 27
Background image, 2, 3, 18–20, 22,
     28–31, 193

C

Cascading Style Sheets (CSS), 23–35
Cloud hosting, 11
Coding errors, 70
Conditional statements, 119
Counter, 129–136
Crosshair cursor, 51, 53, 81, 100
CSSOM View Module, 212

D

delay() method, 139
Depth levels, 163–171
Depths and click zones, 157–171
div, 17, 45, 94, 111
do/while loop, 102
duration function, 68

E

easeInOutQuad, 98
easeInSine, 98
easeOutQuart, 98
Easing function, 97, 98, 145
Eclipse, 6
Embedding, 3, 225–244
e.pageX and e.pageY
     properties, 212

F

File, 6–14, 226–244
Fireworks, 50
Fixed, 26, 35
for/in loops, 102
Frames per second (fps), 68

© Zarrar Chishti 2017
Z. Chishti, *Cross Over to HTML5 Game Development*,
https://doi.org/10.1007/978-1-4842-3291-0

Get the eBook for only $5!

Why limit yourself?

With most of our titles available in both PDF and ePUB format, you can access your content wherever and however you wish—on your PC, phone, tablet, or reader.

Since you've purchased this print book, we are happy to offer you the eBook for just $5.

To learn more, go to http://www.apress.com/companion or contact support@apress.com.

Apress®

Printed in the United States
By Bookmasters